Life and Death in Early Rural Otago

The archaeology and bioarchaeology of St. John's Burial Ground Milton, Otago, New Zealand

PETER PETCHEY AND HALLIE BUCKLEY

With contributions by
Jane Batcheller, Charlotte King, and Rod Wallace

BAR INTERNATIONAL SERIES 3102 | 2022

BAR
PUBLISHING

Published in 2022 by
BAR Publishing, Oxford, UK

BAR International Series 3102

Life and Death in Early Rural Otago

ISBN 978 1 4073 6007 2 paperback
ISBN 978 1 4073 6008 9 e-format

DOI https://doi.org/10.30861/9781407360072
A catalogue record for this book is available from the British Library

COVER IMAGE *St. John's Cemetery, Back Road, Milton, New Zealand. One of the eight standing headstones in the cemetery (Peter Petchey).*

BAR
PUBLISHING

BAR titles are available from:

BAR Publishing
122 Banbury Rd, Oxford, OX2 7BP, UK
info@barpublishing.com
www.barpublishing.com

OF RELATED INTEREST

The Archaeology and Architecture of Farm Buildings at Saumarez Station, Armidale, New South Wales
Graham Connah
BAR International Series **3067** | 2021

Who Came to Tea at the Old Kinchega Homestead?
Tablewares, Teawares and Social Interaction at an Australian Outback Pastoral Homestead
Penelope M. Allison and Virginia Esposito
BAR International Series **2964** | 2020

Henry's Mill: The Historical Archaeology of a Forest Community
Life around a timber mill in south-west Victoria, Australia, in the early twentieth century
Peter Davies
BAR International Series **1558** | 2006

A Critical Exploration of Frameworks for Assessing the Significance of New Zealand's Historic Heritage
Sara Donaghey
BAR International Series **1836** | 2008

The Same under a Different Sky?
A country estate in nineteenth-century New South Wales
Graham Connah
BAR International Series **1625** | 2007

Imperialist Archaeology in the Canary Islands
French and German Studies on Prehistoric Colonization at the End of the 19th Century
A. José Farrujia de la Rosa
BAR International Series **1333** | 2005

Archaeological Excavations at the Uxbridge Almshouse Burial Ground in Uxbridge, Massachusetts
Edited by Ricardo J. Elia and Al B. Wesolowsky
BAR International Series **564** | 1991

Birds of a Feather
Osteological and archaeological papers from the South Pacific in honour of R.J. Scarlett
Edited by Atholl Anderson
BAR International Series **62** | 1979

Acknowledgements

Funding for this excavation was provided by a Grant-in-Aid from the Department of Anatomy, University of Otago, and further analysis has been paid for under a Royal Society of New Zealand Marsden Fund Grant. We are grateful to Wayne Stevenson for the donation of his time and use of his digger. This project is a collaboration between many individuals and groups. The TP60 group who instigated the work at St. Johns Cemetery and provided a vast amount of background research are Robert Findlay, Kath Croy, Isobel Michelle, Mary-Anne Miller and Rev. Vivienne Galletly. Bishop Kelvin Wright has supported the project wholeheartedly, and provided his permission for the excavation to be undertaken. Megan Callaghan, the Health Protection Officer at Public Health South guided us through the disinterment licence process. Rachel Wesley provided Māori cultural guidance, and participated in the excavation. Jane Batcheller of the university of Alberta carried out the fabric analysis, and Rod Wallace of Auckland performed the coffin timber identifications. Richard Walter and Phil Latham of the Department of Archaeology and Anthropology provided much of the excavation and field equipment. Grant Love, who farms the area surrounding the cemetery, has put up with several years of disruptions. Dudley Finch provided material assistance and loaned the A&P show medal.

The field crew were: Baylee Smith, Alana Kelly, Caitlin Hyde, Teina Tutaki, Eleanor Moore, Shar Briden, Stacey Ward, Lori Bowers, Anna-Claire Barker, Rebecca Adam, Naomi Woods, Koreana Wesley-Evans, Sarah McDonald, Gail Elliot, Kath Croy, Anna Willis, Rebecca Kinaston, Greg Hil, Jonny Geber, Rachel Wesley, Nyssa Mildwaters, Jenni Lane, Holly Brinsdon, Jitlada Innanchai, Charlotte King, Kate Domett, Peter Petchey, Hallie Buckley.

Table of Contents

List of figures

List of tables

Abstract

In November-December 2016 the Southern Cemeteries Archaeological Project (a collaboration between the University of Otago and Southern Archaeology Ltd.) carried out an archaeological excavation at the St. John's Cemetery near Milton in Otago, New Zealand. The purpose of this investigation was twofold: to assist a local community group with research into and management of the cemetery; and to investigate the lives, health and burial traditions of early European settlers in New Zealand.

The St. John's Cemetery was established in 1860 by the Church of England to serve the local farming community, it was last used in 1926, and it was formally closed in 1971. In 2014 a local community group, Tokomairiro Project 60 (TP60), was formed with the intention to repair the remaining headstones, to identify the extent of graves (which were suspected to extend beyond the existing fenced area), and ultimately create a well-maintained lawn cemetery. The TP60 group contacted Peter Petchey and Hallie Buckley to seek assistance and the outcome was an opportunity to investigate an early farming community from archaeological and bioarchaeological perspectives.

One of the current themes in New Zealand historical archaeology is the examination of identity, and how this is expressed in the archaeological record. Recent work by historians has examined the British origins of many early settlers, and how they adapted to their new home. New Zealand was often portrayed as offering opportunities for a healthier and more prosperous future than life in Britain, but was this the experience of the early settlers on the Tokomairiro Plain? Were those born and raised in New Zealand healthier than their immigrant parents? The Southern Cemeteries Archaeological Project has sought to address these questions through a combination of historical research, archaeological investigation and bioarchaeological analysis.

The excavation at St Johns Cemetery exposed a total of 29 grave cuts and excavated 25 graves to recover the remains of 27 individuals. Of these four were identified, and this combined with the evidence of coffin style and decoration indicated that most of the individuals who were investigated were buried in the 1870s. All had been buried in wooden coffins, sharing a common basic fashion, with most covered in black fabric and edged with 'coffin lace' (an embossed lead/ tin alloy ribbon), and some also fitted with cast iron handles.

The preservation of the human remains was highly variable across the site, partly due to the variable ground conditions. The condition of the skeletons ranged from completely intact to nothing preserved but the dentition. However, a sufficient sample was retrieved to begin to consider this population in some detail. The breakdown of age and sex found was; 10 infants, 4 children (over 1 year of age and less than 15 years); 1 adolescent/young adult and 11 adults. Amongst the adults 5 were female, 5 were male and 2 could not be determined.

All of the adults had very poor dental health, with high rates of caries and loss of teeth prior to death, either from massive caries or periodontal disease, or both. Cavities were also observed in the teeth of some of the young children. Tuberculosis was common, and one individual that died from this infection was identified. Traumatic injuries were observed in three of the seven well-preserved adults. While the sample is small, this is a very high frequency of trauma. Most of these bone fractures occurred well before death, as shown by evidence of healing, although one individual appears to have died in a serious accident.

Overall the population sample appears to have brought much of their biosocial landscape to New Zealand with them, with both their general health and their funerary traditions reflecting their (mostly) British Isles origins. However, elements of an improving quality of life were also emerging: infant mortality rates in this period were slowly improving, ownership of smallholdings provided some security for some families, community organisations provided formal or informal safety nets, and no-one had an obvious 'paupers burial.'

Introduction

Life in mid nineteenth century New Zealand was tough for many. Māori were experiencing a world of land dispossession and disease epidemics, while early European settlers were learning to live in a new land with unfamiliar geographical and environmental conditions where they had to carve out an existence for themselves and their families (Holland 2013; Petchey 2018; West 2017). Medical science was just beginning to become recognisably modern, as germ theory gradually replaced miasma theory only in the last decades of the nineteenth century. Mortality rates were high from diseases such as tuberculosis. Childbirth was dangerous for both mothers and babies and injury from accidents, especially on farms and in mines, was common. Drowning was known as the 'New Zealand Death' as it was so common (Ell and Ell 1995: 8). Life in New Zealand was promoted as being better than in the British Isles (Figure 1.1), with healthier

living and greater opportunities (Belich 1996: 297-312), but was this actually the case?

Historical sources can tell us much about the experiences of people in this period, but records were often only kept by the literate and those with time to spare or a world view to promote (Ballantyne 2012: 154; Campbell 2013: 2). To understand the lives of those who did not leave a record behind we must turn to the archaeological record, and the best way to understand many aspects of past lives is to look at the people themselves. Beginning in 2016, Peter Petchey and Hallie Buckley of the University of Otago have been directing a bioarchaeological research project that is studying early European burials in cemeteries in Otago: the Southern Cemeteries Archaeological Project. By using a combination of archaeological interpretation of the burial traditions and associated material culture,

Fig. 1.1. A contemporary cartoon showing the idealised vision of life in the colonies compared with life in the British cities. This was the promise that brought many settlers to New Zealand (*Punch*, 1850, Alexander Turnbull Library).

and analysis of the human remains (including osteological assessment of the remains and chemical and molecular analyses), a detailed picture can be built up of the lives of the individuals: an account of their 'lived experiences.' This integrated analysis can provide details of their origins, childhood and adult health, diet, trauma, exposure to environmental toxins, and in some cases the final cause of death. By building detailed osteobiographies of individual early settlers and combining these with archaeological and historical research we can begin to understand how they experienced the New Zealand of the mid nineteenth century both individually and at a wider scale as members of local communities and as part of an evolving colonial society.

In 2016 the Project carried out an archaeological excavation at the old St. John's Cemetery on Back Road, near Milton in Otago (Figure 1.2, Figure 1.3). The site code used here is 'SJM' for 'St John's Milton.' The excavations had a dual purpose: to collaborate with a local community group to assist in their efforts to research and restore the cemetery, and to undertake a bioarchaeological investigation into the past lives and health of this early European farming population.

St. John's Cemetery is an historic Anglican cemetery (Archaeological site H45/56) that was formally established in 1860 but was probably in informal use three years earlier, has been disused since 1926, and was officially closed in 1971. Records located to date indicate that at least 75 people have been buried there, but only eight headstones and marked graves remain today (Figure 1.4, Figure 1.5). By the second decade of the 21st century the cemetery had been in a state of disrepair for many years, and a number of descendants of those buried there formed a community group, the Tokomairiro Project 60 (TP60) with the intention of restoring the graveyard (the '60' was a reference to the number of graves thought to be present when the group was first formed, a figure that soon increased as historical research progressed). One particular problem that the TP60 group faced was the uncertainty of the cemetery boundaries, as the existing fence had been installed in the 1950s or 1960s around the visible headstones, but it was suspected that there were unmarked graves outside of that area.

The intentions of the TP60 group were to repair the remaining headstones (which was completed with the help of the Historic Cemeteries Conservation Trust), to identify the extent of graves within the cemetery and ultimately create a well-maintained lawn cemetery. They also carried out extensive research into the history of the cemetery and those known to be buried there, which was collated into a single volume (Findlay et al 2015). The task of identifying the locations of unmarked graves, and in particular those suspected to be outside the cemetery fence, proved to be problematic as remote sensing options were too expensive for an unfunded community group,

Fig. 1.2. The location of Milton in South Otago

Fig. 1.3. The location of the St. John's Cemetery on Back Road near Milton (NZTopo50 CF15 Milton, Toitū Te Whenua Land Information New Zealand).

and the results of such surveys can be equivocal without some degree of ground-truthing (i.e. confirmation of the results by excavation).

To address this issue the group contacted Dr Petchey and Professor Buckley to seek assistance in defining the

actual cemetery boundary and finding 'lost' graves using archaeological methods. The outcome was a collaboration between the descendant community group and academic researchers that provided an opportunity to investigate an early farming community from archaeological, bioarchaeological and social history perspectives.

Fig. 1.4. The St. Johns Cemetery seen from Back Road in 2016.

Fig. 1.5. Some of the gravestones in the St. John's Cemetery in 2016. No marked graves were investigated during the archaeological excavations.

After extensive public consultation, an archaeological authority (No. 2017/171) from Heritage New Zealand and a disinterment licence (No. 17-2016/17) from the Ministry of Health were obtained, and the Anglican Church (still the landowner) gave its permission for the disinterments. The archaeological excavation of part of the cemetery took place between 28 November and 16 December 2016. The excavation was preceded by a brief blessing by Bishop Kelvin Wright and whakawātea by Rachel Wesley (Te Rūnanga o Ōtākou Ngāi Tahu) on 27 November, and closed by a blessing by the local Vicar, Rev. Vivienne Galletly, on 16 December. Each time a new burial was found (generally at the point where the top of the coffin was identified) Rev. Galletly gave a brief service at the graveside. In cases where individuals were not exhumed (generally due to very poor bone preservation) Rev. Galletly gave a burial service prior to the grave being backfilled. The traditional Anglican burial service, as these people would have known it was used (all burials that we could date were from the 1870s).

Research Questions

One current theme in New Zealand historical archaeology is the examination of identity, and how this is expressed in the archaeological record (Campbell and Furey 2013; Jones 2012; Petchey and Brosnahan 2016; Smith 2004, 2008, 2019). Given the status of New Zealand as a British colony after the signing of the Treaty of Waitangi in 1840 it is hardly surprising that the majority of immigrants settlers were of British Isles origin, and recent work by historians has examined these settlers and how they adapted to their new home (Andrews 2009; Fraser and McCarthy 2012; Holland 2013; Palenski 2012; Phillips and Hearn 2008; West 2017). Similarly, the overwhelming majority of archaeological material culture found in historic New Zealand sites has been of British origin, albeit with some material also coming from Australia, the US, Europe and China, reflecting the increasingly global trade networks of this period and the presence of Chinese miners in the goldfields from the mid-1860s (Bedford1986: 19-89; Petchey and Innanchai 2012; Prickett 1994: 38-85; Ritchie 1997: 120-123; Smith 2019: 263).

From the mid-nineteenth century entrepreneurial shipping and land companies promoted migration to New Zealand not only to the poor, but also to the middle classes (who had money to invest) with promises of land and opportunity. New Zealand was portrayed as offering opportunities for a healthier and more prosperous future than life in the British Isles (Belich 1996: 279, 297-312; Burns 1989; Harper 2012: 42; Phillips and Hearn 2008: 23-25; West 2017: 162), but was this the experience of the early settlers on the Tokomairiro Plain? Were those born and raised in New Zealand healthier than their immigrant parents? While historical research can answer some questions about the early settlers around Milton, historical records can be incomplete, misleading or simply incorrect (Ballantyne 2012: 154; Campbell 2013: 2), and many aspects of the early settlers' origins, health, diet and family associations are better able to be addressed through a combination of historical research, archaeological investigation and bioarchaeological analysis.

Bioarchaeology is the analysis of human skeletal remains from archaeological sites, and is uniquely placed to address questions about the biological life histories of these early settlers. A variety of analytical techniques can be used to examine the lives of these individuals, including macroscopic examination of the bones and teeth integrated with chemical and molecular information on origins, diet and disease (Buikstra and Ubelaker 1994; Hillson 1996; Katzenberg and Saunders 2008; Larsen 2002; Price et al 2002). The exhumation of graves and analysis of human skeletal remains from historic cemeteries has been carried out in Britain and Europe (e.g. Brickley and Buteux 2006; Miles and Connell 2012), the US and a small number in Australia (e.g. Anson and Henneberg 2004; Owen and Casey 2017; Owen, Casey and Pitt 2017; Donlon, Griffin and Casey 2017, Gurr et al. 2022). In the United Kingdom, where many of New Zealand's colonial settlers originated, this work has established the biosocial context of lived experiences during the Industrial Revolution in urban and rural settings and compared the health effects of increasing industrialisation between the two contexts (e.g. Gowland et al. 2018a). Recurring themes are of increased hardship and detrimental health effects amongst the urban poor and a relatively 'healthier' lifestyle in rural settings (Roberts and Cox 2003). Families of higher social standing and greater wealth were afforded better access to state support, which resulted in better health and this may be reflected in the bioarchaeological record (Mays et al. 2009). Within this setting of industrialisation and marked social hierarchy there was a push for Empire-building involving immigration to new colonies, including New Zealand (Ballantyne 2012; Burns 1989). The 17th-19th century colonial drive by Europeans to new lands already settled by Indigenous peoples had devastating consequences for those existing populations, some of which were intentional, such as marginalisation from ancestral lands, while others were unintentional such as the introduction of new infectious diseases (Pool 1991, 2015).

Examination of mortuary ritual, and in particular gravestone design, has been a fruitful subject for many years (e.g. Deed 2015, Deetz 1967, Mytum 2003). Above-ground study is reasonably straightforward, and there has been recent detailed research on New Zealand cemetery design and meaning (Deed 2015). Subsurface archaeological excavation of cemeteries is more involved and complex, and raises many ethical issues with regard to the disturbance of human remains. Work that has been done has allowed the buried trappings of Victorian funerary practice to be examined, and there is a growing international body of information about burial practice and coffin furniture (e.g. Brickley and Buteux 2006; Hoile 2018; Miles and Connell 2012), although until the present research was carried out there was very limited archaeological information regarding New Zealand practice. While bioarchaeological analysis may be able to determine the origins and health of the interred individuals, consideration of the funerary practices can also help shed light on their cultural identity and how this was expressed in a new home. In the present research only unmarked graves have been investigated, and so there is no headstone information; all archaeological evidence of funerary practices is from within the graves.

By combining the bioarchaeological and archaeological evidence of the life and death of individuals interred in the St. Johns Cemetery with a wider consideration of the archaeological landscape and historical community that they inhabited when alive, it is possible to build a picture of their world and their agency and understanding within it. This is attempted here by undertaking two longitudinal case studies of individuals from the cemetery, considering their origins, move to New Zealand, families and community relationships.

The excavation at St. John's Cemetery is a combined research- and community- driven project that combines a variety of analyses of the human remains, an archaeological interpretation of both the funerary practices at the cemetery and the wider archaeological landscape that these people inhabited, and a detailed study of the social history of several of the individuals, to build up a comprehensive picture of these people and their community. This is the first time that such a research programme has been attempted on an early European population in New Zealand.

History of St. Johns Cemetery

The Otago settlement, in the south of New Zealand's South Island, was a joint venture between the Lay Association of the Free Church of Scotland and the New Zealand Company, which acquired 144,600 acres of land in coastal Otago from Ngāi Tahu in 1844. The intention was to establish a Wakefield class settlement, where the community would be divided into a land-owning capitalist class, and a wage-earning working class (Hocken 1898; Olssen 1984; Schrader 2016). Land in the settlement was divided into urban, suburban and rural property, with the intention that agriculture would develop in the hinterland. In this period New Zealand was promoted as a land of plenty to encourage families to settle and develop the growing colony, and one of the attractions of schemes such as the Otago settlement was the opportunity to own land.

The first two ships carrying settlers, the *John Wickliffe* and the *Philip Laing*, arrived in March and April 1848 respectively, with 97 and 247 emigrants aboard (Hocken 1898:94; Olssen 1984:33). Initial growth was slow, and in October 1848 the Rev. Thomas Burns recorded the population of Dunedin and the surrounding areas as 444 Europeans and 166 Māori (Hocken 1898:106). But Dunedin's fortunes changed in 1861 when the first of the major Otago gold rushes occurred at Gabriel's Gully, followed by the larger Dunstan Rush in 1862 (Olssen 1984; Salmon 1963). These events brought a massive influx of people and capital to Dunedin, and the population rose from 2262 in 1859 to 15,790 in 1864 (McDonald 1965:44, 51). The gold mining powered a commercial boom in the city and wider province, but it was the establishment of farming that was essential for the long-term viability of settlement. The fledgling city of Dunedin needed a productive hinterland to provide food, and the easily won gold soon ran out leaving the miners two options: move on or settle down. The first settlers on the Tokomairiro Plain arrived there in 1850, by 1857 a flour mill was at work with a fledgling community growing up close by, and in 1860 this settlement was formally surveyed and named 'Milton' (Sumpter and Lewis 1949). Sumpter and Lewis (1949: 13) stated that most of the early settlers on the Tokomairiro were Scottish, but the English were always a notable presence in the early Otago settlement; tensions between the Presbyterian Scots and the Anglican English led to some of the latter being dubbed the 'Little Enemy' by the former (McDonald 1965: 19).

The local Resident Magistrate in the Tokomairiro district was John Dewe, who owned land at what would later be known as Jones Bush. It was at his home that the first Church of England services in the district were held in the late 1850s (Fraser 1941: 3; Sumpter and Lewis 1949: 52). The local Anglican community was clearly of some

size by this time, as Bishop Chitty-Harper of the Diocese of Christchurch (which at that time included a vast area, including Tokomairiro) visited in July 1858 and celebrated the Holy Communion to a congregation of 70 people, baptised three infants and confirmed six people (Fraser 1941: 3-4; Sumpter and Lewis 1949: 52).

A priority for early communities was the establishment of Churches of various denominations, but equally necessary for obvious pragmatic reasons were burial grounds (Deed 2015: 56). Not only did disease cause many fatalities, but there were many other hazards of colonial life including drowning (often termed the 'New Zealand death' due to the high rates of death at stream and river crossings in particular), and accidents with stock (in particular horse falls and kicks) (*Bruce Herald* 13 July 1865, 19 February 1868, 27 January 1874; Ell and Ell 1995:159; *Lake County Press* 31 December 1885; *Otago Witness* 1 February 1894). At Tokomairiro John Dewe donated an acre of land (Part section 93 Block XI Tokomairiro) to the Anglican Church for a cemetery and chapel, this being the St. Johns Cemetery that is the subject of this report. The first known burials there were in 1857 (an un-named child of William Henning Mansford) and 1859 (Alex Dudgeon McDonald, aged 55) (Tokomairiro Burial Records, Department of Internal Affairs). The Title Deed records the formal land transfer for the token sum of ten shillings in 1860 and the chapel and cemetery were consecrated by Bishop Chitty-Harper on 9 March 1860 (Otago Deeds 4/491; Sumpter and Lewis 1949: 52).

The first cadastral survey of the wider area had been carried out in 1847 by Drake and Watts, contract surveyors (S.O. 80), and this does not show the cemetery (as it pre-dates its use), but the cemetery does appear on an 1880 plan (D.P. 259) which shows the 1 acre 8 perches (4248 sq.m.) 'English Cemetery' on Back Road, surrounded by a gorse fence (Figure 3.1). The only known plan of the cemetery (Figure 3.3) is undated and contains only seven names handwritten into plots: the identities of early burials are discussed further below. The formal layout and presence of a chapel places the cemetery into what Deed (2015: 134) defines as 'churchyard burial grounds,' a rural colonial continuation of the British tradition of graveyard placement that had already been replaced in Britain by the development of large modern cemeteries and the legislated closure of church graveyards from the 1850s onwards.

At this stage the parish did not yet have a vicar, but it was felt that a Parsonage and glebe (a piece of land that was provided for a clergyman to provide support and income) would be essential to attract one. Bishop Chitty-Harper purchased a 26 acre block of land (part of Section

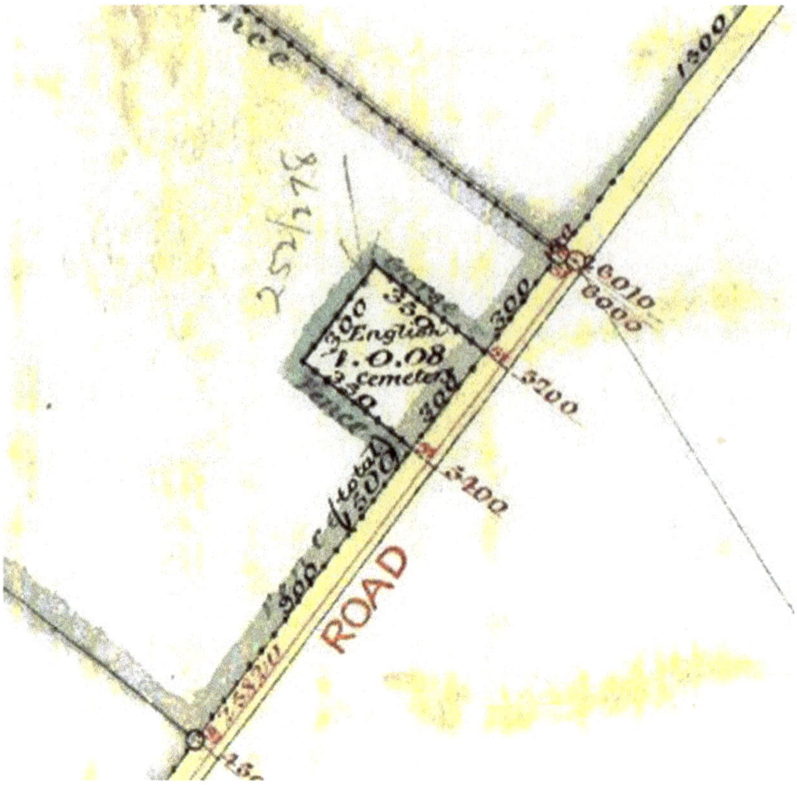

Fig. 3.1. Detail from an 1880 map of part of Block XI Tokomairiro District by surveyor Alexander Adam. This shows the 'English Cemetery' on Back Road, with an area of just over one acre (Otago DP 259, Crown Copyright, Toitū Te Whenua Land Information New Zealand).

Fig. 3.2. The old Church of England Parsonage near the St. Johns Cemetery (Sumpter and Lewis 1949).

86 Block X Tokomairiro Dictrict) on the opposite side of Back Road from the cemetery from James Crane for £250 (Otago Deeds 29/232) (ownership passed to the Dunedin Diocesan Trust Board in 1885). John Dewe was again instrumental in raising funds for the erection of a house on this land, and in 1859 the Church of England Parsonage Fund was raising money for this purpose (*Otago Witness* 26 February 1859). The missing element was still a minister, and money was also raised to pay for the passage from England for the Reverend R.L. Standford, late junior curate at St. Michael's, Coventry, who arrived in Milton in November 1864 (Fraser 1941: 5). His new home was a weatherboard house set well back from the road on the 26 acre glebe: the only known photographs of the house show it after additions were made in 1869, by which time it was a two storey timber weatherboard building with six windows and a veranda to the front (Figure 3.2). The

St. Johns Parish Burial Register records that John Dewe officiated at most interments up until late 1864, and the first burial ceremony performed by the Rev. Standford was on Christmas Day 1864, the month after he arrived in Milton (Burial Register, entry no. 20, Caroline Webb).

However, at the same time as the Church of England cemetery was established a public cemetery was also opened nearby at Fairfax (Cemetery Reserves Ordinance 1864). Only a few years later the Anglican chapel became redundant after the Otago gold rushes of the early 1860s drew the road traffic away from Back Road and along the more direct route through Milton. By the time the Rev. Standford, arrived in 1864 the parishioners were already planning to build a new church in the township. After issues with site suitability (the first site selected would have required expensive foundations) and costs (the first design selected through a competition was too expensive to build) a new brick church was erected in the township in 1866, with John Dewe laying the foundation stone in January that year (Fraser 1941: 7; Sumpter and Lewis 1949: 52). The exact fate of the old Back Road chapel is difficult to determine: it was probably sold for removal from the cemetery site, and later destroyed by fire. Fraser (1941: 16) stated: 'according to the minute book of the Vestry it was sold to Mr. Hare for £7 in 1883, the old harmonium being brought to Milton for Sunday School use. It was later destroyed by fire.' Another source states that it was removed to Clarendon in about 1868 (Findlay et al 2015).

The use of the old St. John's Cemetery had also declined in favour of the Fairfax Cemetery, and by 1898 the cemetery trust was requesting that it be closed. According to the St John's Parish Burial Register only five burials were undertaken after 1900. The last known burial was of John Moore in 1926, and the cemetery ground fell into disrepair and the boundaries were lost. The cemetery was formally closed in 1971 and the control and management was vested to the Dunedin Diocesan Trust Board. The area of marked graves was fenced off (although as the archaeological investigations would prove, unmarked graves were present over a wider area), and the balance of the land was leased to a local farmer, who built a hayshed where the chapel had stood.

Distance from Milton also determined the fate of the old Parsonage. By the 1870s it had become clear that it was too far away from the town and the new church, and the Vicar (by then the Rev. Richard Coffey) moved into Milton: one account states that he simply refused to live in the old Parsonage. The old house was rented out, the income being used to offset the Vicar's accommodation

expenses (Fraser 1941: 14; Mackintosh 1966: 8). A new Vicarage was designed by Rev. Geoffrey Fynnes Clinton and built beside the St. John's Church in Milton in 1886 (Fraser 1941: 18; Mackintosh 1966: 9), which continued to be used for its intended purpose until the retirement of the Rev. Vivienne Galletly in 2017, and it was sold in 2019. By 1966 the old Parsonage was described as derelict (Mackintosh 1966: 4), and it was later demolished and a new farmhouse built just beside where the old house had stood.

3.1. St. John's Cemetery: Early Interments

There are no surviving detailed records of who is buried in the St. John's Cemetery. The TP60 group have been endeavouring to create a complete list (Findlay et al 2015), but there are many uncertainties. The 2016 archaeological investigation found the broken headstone for Henry Pim who died in 1872, and for whom there is no record of his having been buried at St. Johns. There are three extant relevant sources: the undated burial plot plan of the cemetery, the Parish Burial Register (both held by the Hocken Archives), and the Tokomairiro Death Registers (Department of Internal Affairs). None are comprehensive, especially for the earliest years. The plan of the cemetery has only seven names written in (Table 3.1), and the Parish Register (Table 3.2) covers a number of cemeteries in the wider area, and early entries do not stipulate which burial was in which cemetery.

There are 124 surveyed plots shown on the cemetery plan (Figure 3.3), and there are estimates of 'about 200 burials' in the graveyard (as stated by the cemetery trustees in 1928, quoted in Findlay et al 2015). As the 2016 archaeological excavations found there are burials outside the 124 surveyed plots, as at least one more row of graves exists along the northern side of the cemetery than is shown in the plan. The TP60 group has found records of 68 burials of known people, yet only seven graves remained marked with headstones in 2016 (Table 4.1).

Table 3.1. Names on the plan of the Church of England Cemetery, Tokomairiro.

Name	Plot number	Comments
Ottrey	3	Very faint pencil
Caudle	61	Very faint pencil
Bugden	64	
J Powley	106	
? Powley	107	Very faded
B (?)	113	Pencil initial
B (?)	114	Pencil initial
B (?)	115	Pencil initial
Jordon	118	
Thomas Parker	119	

Table 3.2. St. John's Parish Burial Register 1ˢᵗ page. The place of interment was not recorded.

No	When Buried	Name and Surname	Age	Name of Parents or Husband	Place of Residence	By Whom Ceremony was Performed
1		Crane		James (?) Crane	Tokomairiro	John Dewe
2		Crane				
3		Smythe	34	Smythe	Tokomairiro	No one
4		Powley				
5		Cockerill				
6		Cockerill				
7		Finch		James Finch	Tokomairiro	J Dewe
8		Cooke	43		Tokomairiro	
9		Bridgeman	1	Thomas and Jane Bridgeman	Tokomairiro	
10	Nov 12 1860	Elizabeth Woodhead	69		Tokomairiro	Revd EJ Edwards
11	May 9 1862	Richard Westbrook Squires	25		Tokomairiro	J Dewe
12	April 17 1864	William Arpe (?)	5		Tokomairiro	J Dewe

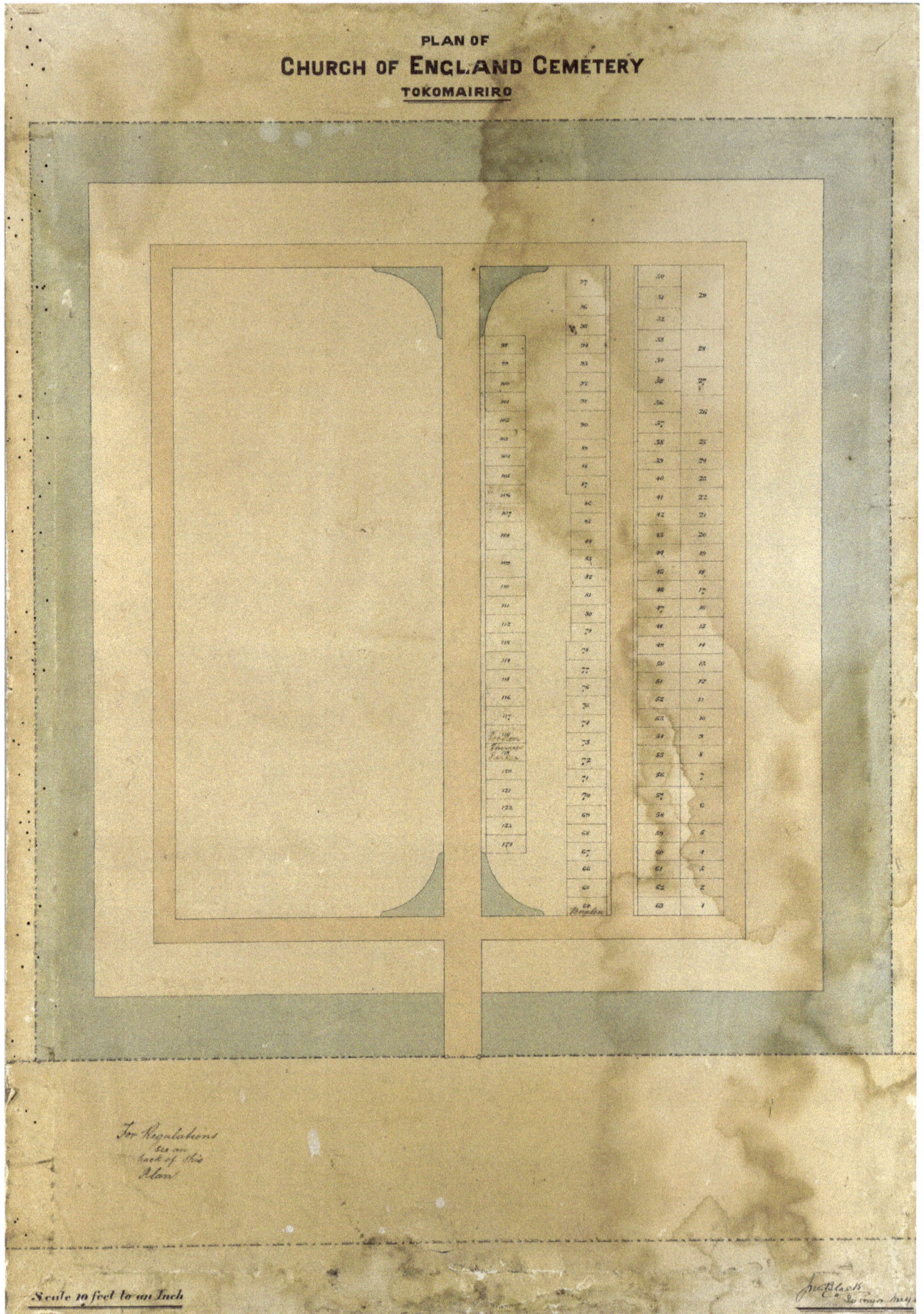

PLAN OF

CHURCH OF ENGLAND CEMETERY

TOKOMAIRIRO

Scale 10 feet to an Inch

Fig. 3.3. The only surviving layout plan for the St. John's Cemetery. It has only seven names written in plots. The unoccupied left hand side of the cemetery is where the chapel stood (and is now occupied by a hay barn) (Hocken Archives, Uare Taoka o Hākena, MS-1875-007).

4

St Johns Cemetery, Site Description

The St. John's Cemetery is situated on Back Road, 1.3km to the east of Milton in Otago, on the edge of the Tokomairiro Plain. The surrounding land is flat open pasture, rising to the coastal hills to the east. The original Church property was a square area of just over one acre beside the road (Figure 3.1 above), and as of 2022 this still remains the property of the Anglican Church. The NE half of the property was laid out in grave plots (Figure 3.3), and a chapel was erected on the SW side, but as described above this was moved after only a few years use. The chapel side of the cemetery property was later leased to the farmer who owned the surrounding land, and in the late 1960s he built the concrete and iron haybarn that still stands approximately where the chapel had stood.

The site as it appeared by the late 2010s is shown in Figure 4.1. A post and wire fence enclosed a slightly irregular area of approximately 26 metres by 45 metres, which contained all of the visible gravestones and unmarked grave depressions. However, this fenceline did not extend to the full extent of the legal cemetery boundary, which was approximately indicated by a partial enclosure of large trees and old stumps. As is described in this report, during the 2016 archaeological investigation a further 16 burials were found in the area outside the fenced enclosure. A farm track ran through the middle of the property from a gate on Back Road, and the haybarn stood on the opposite side of the track from the fenced graveyard.

There were eight headstones/marked graves still present prior to the 2016 excavations (Figure 4.3, Figure 4.4, Figure 4.5), and during the investigation one further broken and buried stone (Figure 4.6) and the footings for a timber grave enclosure were found. The surviving stones are a mixture of standing tablets and horizontal slabs. The TP60 Group in collaboration with the Historic Cemeteries Conservation Trust has repaired much of the damage to the stones (apart from the one found in 2016). These marked graves were given 'stone' numbers by Findlay et al (2015), and their numbering is repeated here (Table 4.1), with the two additional marked graves identified by their Burial numbers in the Archaeological excavation sequence (Table 4.1).

The layout of burials as suggested by the extant gravestones and the grave shaft depressions that were visible in the ground (Figure 4.2), and as confirmed by the

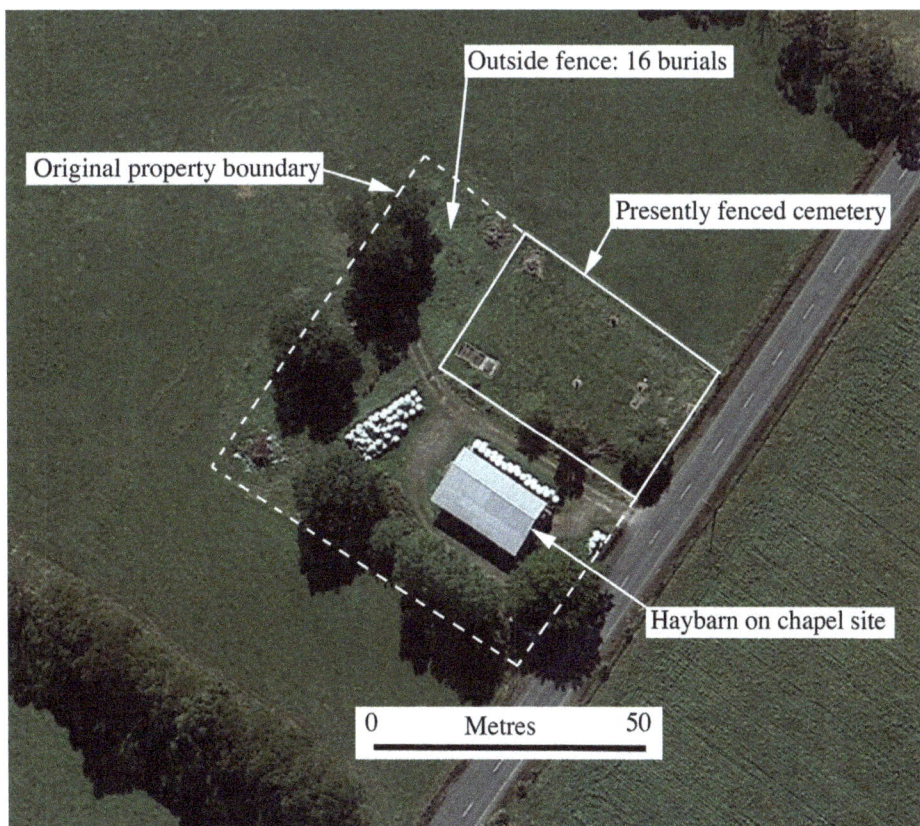

Fig. 4.1. The St. John's Cemetery site, showing the approximate original boundary, the present fenceline and the haybarn that stands approximately where the chapel original stood (Map data: Google Earth, with annotations).

Table 4.1. Headstones and marked graves. TP60 numbering is used for the standing stones ('Stone' numbers), and 2016 Burial numbers are used for marked graves identified during the archaeological excavation.

Marker No.	Name and date	Description
Stone 1	Fanny Fynes-Clinton, 1888	Celtic cross tablet.
Stone 2	John Finch, 1897, Elizabeth Finch, 1875, William Finch, 1875	Polished red granite slab set in concrete base (prob. Not original stone).
Stone 3	No name	Concrete perimeter low wall with cast iron fence (damaged)
Stone 4	Richard Westbrook Squires, 1862	Limestone tablet.
Stone 5	Robert Miller, 1863	White marble tablet.
Stone 6	Richard Pilkington, 1877	Limestone slab.
Stone 7	Joseph Clegg, 1877, Mary Clegg, 1880	Pink granite tablet.
Stone 8	John Clegg, 1876	Limestone tablet.
Burial 11	Unknown, but suspected to be Joseph Higgins, 1877	Four timber post butts for grave enclosure found in 2016. No headstone.
Burial 12	Henry Pim, 1872	Limestone tablet (broken) found in 2016.

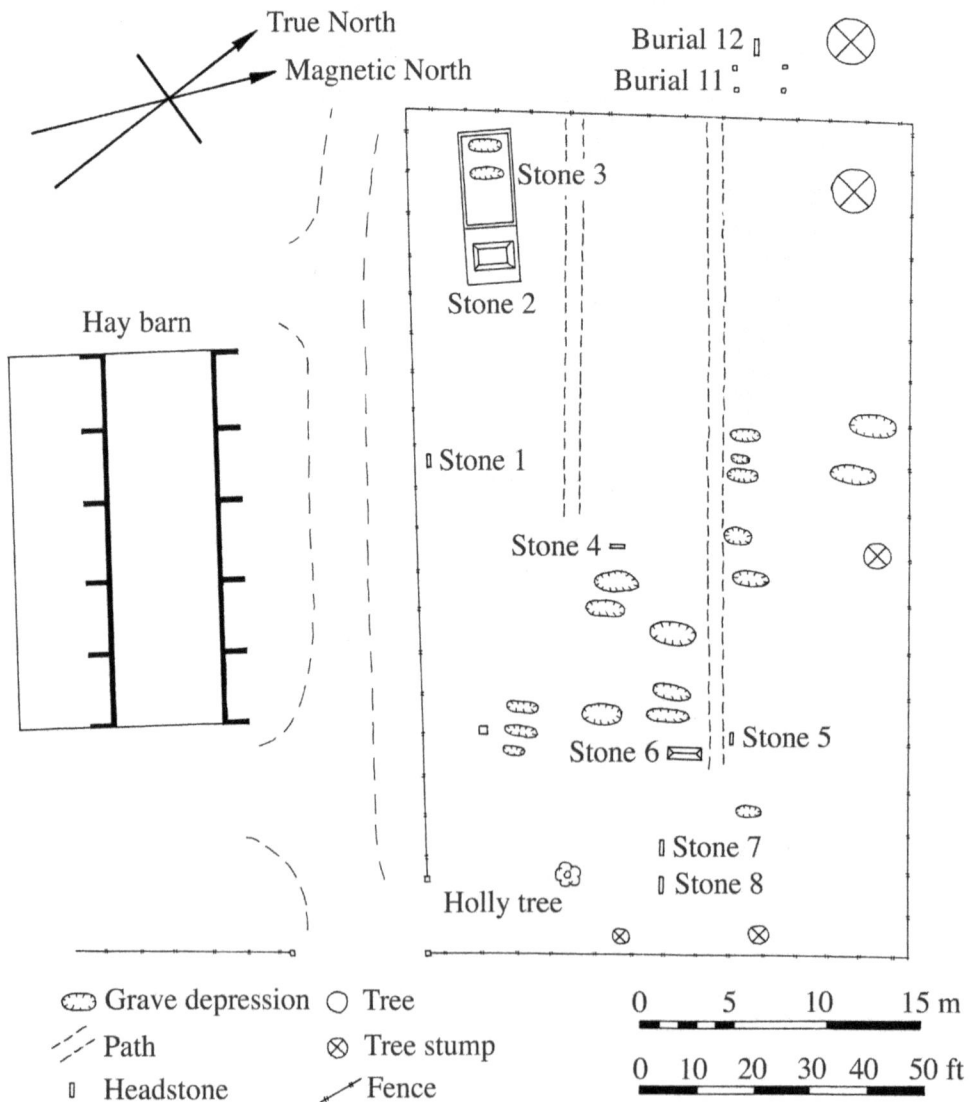

Fig. 4.2. Plan of marked graves in St. John's Cemetery. Note that the locations of Burials 11 and 12 were only found during the archaeological investigations; previously a fragment of the Burial 12 headstone was lying on the surface nearby.

12

Fig. 4.3. The horizontal slab for the Finch family members (front, Stone 2), and the un-named enclosure (rear, Stone 3).

Fig. 4.4. The gravestone for Richard Westbrooke Squires who died in 1862 aged 24 years (Stone 4).

13

Fig. 4.5. The horizontal stone for Richard Pilkington who died in 1877 (Stone 6).

Fig. 4.6. Henry Pim's headstone being held in place by Alana Kelly and Teina Tutaki after it was found during topsoil stripping. Prior to the discovery of this headstone there was no record of Pim having been buried in this cemetery. He died in 1872 at the age of just 34. The grave was recorded as Burial 12, but was not further investigated in 2016.

2016 archaeological excavations (Figure 5.2), followed reasonably closely the formal plot layout as shown in the surviving plan (Figure 3.3) with rows of burials laid out along two paths that ran perpendicular to the Back Road frontage, but with the addition of one or two extra rows along the northern side of the cemetery, and several graves beyond the western extent of the surveyed plots. While the traditional orientation for a Christian cemetery is an east-west alignment of the graves (with the head at the western end) the formalised layout of the cemetery aligned with the cadastral boundaries means that the graves are orientated NE-SW (or closer to north-south magnetic). There is no evidence whether there was any denominational divisions in the cemetery, but as this was known as the Church of England Cemetery and the secular Fairfax Cemetery was opened at the same time it is likely that other denominations were buried there.

Overall, the St John's Cemetery on Back Road was a well-ordered graveyard typical of settled rural communities of the period (Deed 2015: 140-141).

5

Excavation Methodology and Results

Excavation was undertaken in three areas (Figure 5.2): the area outside of the existing cemetery fence (Area 1), the parallel area on the south side of the central farm track (Area 2), and an area within the fenced cemetery that had grave depressions but no headstones (Area 3). All of these areas were inside the legal boundaries of the cemetery, but only Area 3 was within the existing cemetery fence. A remote sensing survey of the cemetery gave no usable results, so a wide area topsoil strip was instead used to identify grave cuts. Excavation was carried out by using a 13 ton digger with a smooth-lipped cleaning bucket to strip back topsoil, at which point most graves cuts could be easily identified. The same machine was used to excavate down around each grave until the level of the coffin was reached, after which work continued by hand (Figure 5.1). Care was taken to prepare the excavation to conform to Worksafe guidelines regarding work within ground excavations, ensuring that excavation sides were battered back and safe depth to width ratios of the excavations were maintained (Worksafe New Zealand 2014). Archaeologists on the team were generally responsible for the excavation of the main grave fill and exposure of coffins and coffin furniture, while the bioarchaeologists exposed, recorded and lifted the human remains.

The site code 'SJM' was used (for 'St Johns Milton'). Each grave cut and each individual interment was given a unique context number, so that in the case of a double interment in one grave there were three context numbers (one for the grave and one for each interment). Only the actual interment context numbers are used in this report (Table 4). No graves with gravestones were investigated.

Fig. 5.1. Careful excavation of the Burial 9 coffin plate (Robert Rowley Thompson) on 2 December 2016. Timber boards were used alongside the excavations to prevent the sides collapsing.

One complicating factor during the digging was the presence of a Telecom telephone line that had been run around the outside of the existing cemetery fence, but (as was discovered) inside the actual area of interments. Chorus (the successor to Telecom as owner of NZ telecommunications infrastructure) kindly moved the phone line at no cost, but its presence complicated the systematic excavation of the site, hence the out-of-sequence numbering of Burials 28 and 29.

A second complication was the high ground water level due to a very wet 2016 spring in Otago, and the variable ground conditions that were encountered. Some of the excavated area was heavy yellow clay, through which ground water hardly passed, but which retained any rainwater that ran into the grave shafts: even after some

140 years the backfill in these graves had not consolidated and tended to be soft and waterlogged. Other parts of the excavated area consisted of gravel, through which the ground water flowed freely. Two burials (Burials 1 and 6) needed to have sumps dug beside the grave cut, and a water pump was used to control the water inflow.

5.1. Excavation Results

The excavation exposed a total of 29 grave cuts (Figure 5.2) and excavated 25 graves to recover the remains of 27 individuals (two of the infant/child burials contained double burials (graves 3A and 3B, and 20A and 20B)). Three grave cuts that were identified after topsoil removal were not excavated due to lack of time (Burials 24, 25, 26). Finally, a broken and buried headstone was found, bearing

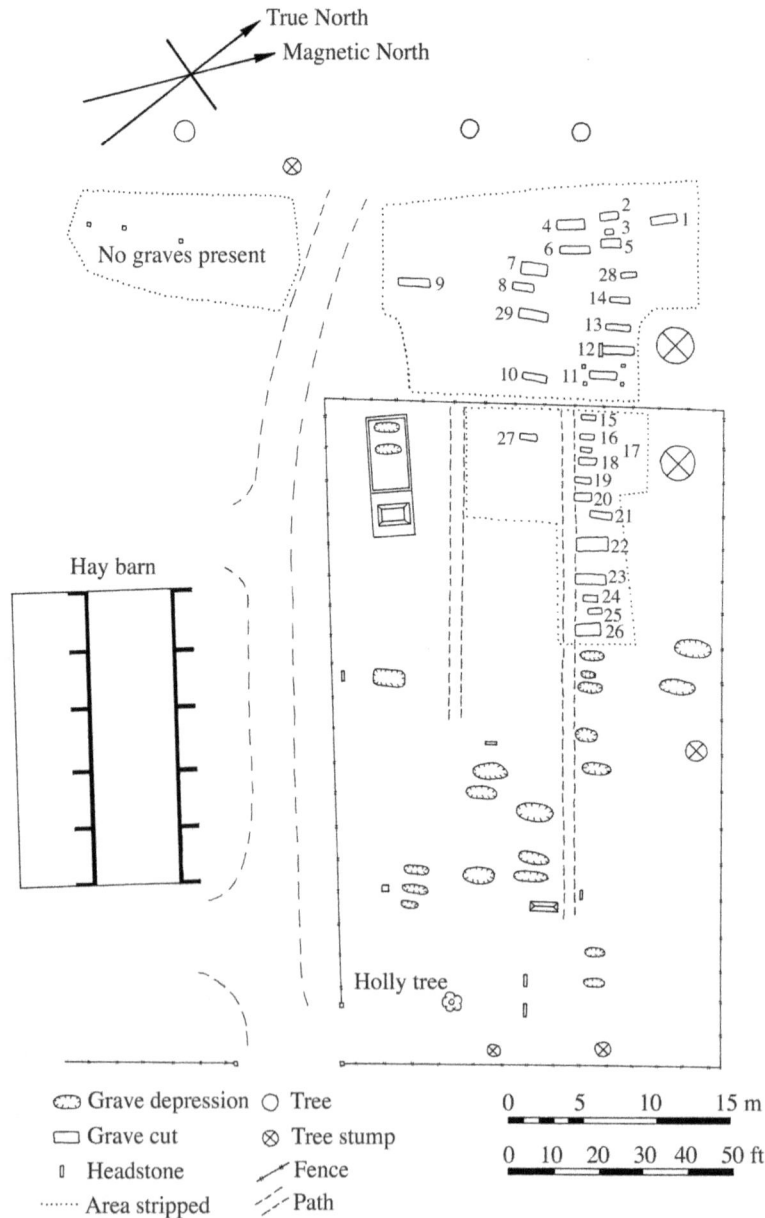

Fig. 5.2. Plan of St. John's Cemetery, showing the results of the 2016 archaeological investigation. The fenced cemetery area is shown bottom right, and the areas that were stripped by machine are indicated. The burials extended 14 metres beyond the existing back fence.

the name of Henry Pim (Figure 4.6), and as the permissions were for unmarked and unidentified burials, this burial (Burial 12) was left untouched. Sixteen graves were found in the area to the rear of the fenced cemetery, confirming everyone's suspicions that the cemetery was larger than the fenced area. The layout of these 'lost' burials continued in the rows from the known cemetery, in particular alongside the northern of the two gravel paths that once ran the length of the graveyard. Notably, the northernmost row, while within the legal cemetery boundary, was outside the formally laid out plots as shown in Figure 3.3.

Most coffins were of the standard 'single break' form, that is wider at the shoulders and tapering towards to head and feet, the shape that is still used for coffins today. All were made of timber.

The preservation of the human remains was highly variable across the site, partly due to the variable ground conditions described above. The condition of the skeletons ranged from completely intact to only the dentition and in one case (Burial 9), no tissues survived. However, a sufficient sample was retrieved to begin to consider in some detail this population. The breakdown of age and sex found was; 10 infants, 4 children (over 1 year of age and less than 15 years); 1 adolescent/young adult and 11 adults. Amongst the adults 5 were female, 5 were male and 2 could not be determined. The burials were all aligned on a north-south (magnetic) axis (aligned with the formally surveyed cemetery plan), and all except one (Burial 19, a child) had the head to the south. These burials are individually described in detail below, and summarised in Table 5.1, followed by a detailed analysis in the following chapter.

Table 5.1. Summary of burials investigated at St. John's Cemetery, Milton, in 2016.

Burial No.	Context No	Grave depth	Orientation (head towards)	Age (est)	Age actual	Sex	Name	Date of death
1	10013	1.6	South	5				
2	10005	1.3	South	Perinate				
3a	10006		South	Perinate				
3b	10016	1.4	South	2.5 yrs				
4	10018	1.63	South		41	M	Dr. Gustavus Weber	1874
5	10012	1.63	South	7-12 yrs				
6	10016	1.9	South		36	F	Flora Weber	1874
7	10014	1.73	South	Old		M?		
8	10058	1.5	South	1.5 yrs				
9	10015	1.82	South		47	M	Robert Rowley Thompson	1877
10	10028	1.8	South	Old		F		
11	10029	1.85	South	Middle age		M	Joseph Higgins?	1877
12	Not exc.				34	M	Henry Pim	1872
13	10026	1.68	South	Middle age?		M		
14	10027	1.4	South	Pre-perinate?				
15	10042	1.35	South	Pre-perinate?				
16	10043	1.45	South	2 yrs		F?	Mary Anne Flahive?	
17	10041	1.1	South	Pre-perinate?				
18	10044	1.4	South	1.5 yrs				
19	10045	1.6	North	1 yr				
20a	10046		South	15 months		F?	Caudle?	1873?
20b	10059	1.5	South	3 yrs		F?	Caudle?	1873?
21	10047	1.9	South		42	M	William Toogood	1873
22	10048	1.8	South	Adult		F?		
23	10049	1.6	South	Adult		F?		
24	Not exc.							
25	Not exc.							
26	Not exc.							
27	10053	1.45	South	15 months				
28	10056	1.1	South	Perinate				
29	10057	1.6	South	Middle age		F		

5.2. Burial 1 (Context No 10013)

Burial 1 (Figure 5.3) was of a ~5 year old child of unknown identity, located in the far NW corner of the cemetery. It was outside the established formal rows of excavated burials, although it lined up with several unexcavated burial depressions in the fenced area of the cemetery. The burial was dug into gravelly soil, through which the ground water passed freely. Old tree roots and evidence of very hot burning indicated that a large tree had previously been located nearby, and had been felled and burnt out. The roots had followed the grave cut down, and had severely disturbed the burial.

The wooden coffin was of the standard single-break form (wider at the shoulders and tapering towards to head and feet), but the tree roots had distorted its shape. It was possible to tell that it was approximately 4 feet 11 inches (1.5m) long, with a maximum width of 14 inches (360mm) at the shoulders. The coffin had been covered in black fabric with embossed lead/tin decorative ribbon. There were fragments of iron coffin plates over the chest and feet, and plain cast iron coffin handles.

There was no survival of the postcranial skeleton. The skull was also not preserved. There was a tree root ball where the cranial vault had been prior to disintegration. The only material present was tooth crowns with most of the dentine (roots and internal crown material) dissolved. Enough of the tooth roots survived in some of the permanent teeth to determine that these were unerupted at death and two of the teeth were deciduous molars that may also have been unerupted. There were no pathological lesions of the remaining teeth present.

Fig. 5.3. Burial 1 after the coffin outline was exposed. The distortion due to tree root damage is clear. The channel at the top of the image was dug to drain the rising groundwater.

5.3. Burial 2 (Context No. 10005)

Burial 2 (Figure 5.4) was a perinatal (around birth; 40 foetal weeks to ~birth) burial of unknown identity in a small fabric-wrapped coffin. The coffin was a miniature

Fig. 5.4. Burial 2 after the top of the coffin was exposed.

form of the standard single-break coffin shape, but was only 28 inches (700mm) long and 10 inches (250mm) wide across the shoulders. The fabric-covered lid was edged in embossed lead/tin ribbon, again in a miniature version of standard adult practice at this cemetery.

The cranium, right pectoral girdle, upper part of the right humerus, parts of the pelvis and the upper half of the femora were preserved in this infant. The skeletal tissue was very friable and did not survive well during the lifting process. A few unidentifiable unerupted deciduous tooth buds were present. One upper central incisor survived well enough to assess the development of the tooth. Some unerupted deciduous teeth were also present in the mandible and revealed through x-ray. Age was estimated based on dental and cranial bone development. A small amount of short (20mm) hair was also preserved. There was no evidence of pathology.

5.4. Burials 3a (Context No. 10006) and 3b (Context No. 10016)

Burials 3a and 3b were of two young children (a perinatal infant and a young child of about 2-3 years) in the same grave, located in the main burial row beside the gravel path, but outside the fenced area of the cemetery. They were both in coffins, buried one on top of the other. The upper coffin contained Burial 3a, the lower coffin contained Burial 3b. The timber of both coffins was poorly preserved, but the small size of the interments meant that the coffin voids had not collapsed.

5.4.1. Burial 3a (Context No. 10006)

Burial 3a (Figure 5.5) was the upper of a pair of infants buried in the same grave (see also Burial 3b). There was no soil between the two coffins, so it is likely that they were buried at the same time.

Burial 3a was a perinatal infant and was interred in a small fabric-wrapped coffin of a miniature single-break form: although the timber had largely decayed away the

Fig. 5.5. Burial 3a in the ground prior to the lid being lifted.

Fig. 5.7. Burial 3b showing the reasonably preserved coffin fabric.

Fig. 5.6. Burial 3a after the coffin lid was lifted off. The femora and tibiae were the best-preserved elements of the skeleton, and can be seen centre left.

fabric remained intact, and the coffin was small enough that its shape had been preserved and the interior void had remained open. The coffin measured 24 inches long and 8 ½ inches wide (660mm by 220mm). The fabric-covered lid was edged in embossed lead/tin ribbon, again in a miniature version of standard adult practice at this cemetery.

The body had been buried lying on the right side with lower limbs flexed and drawn up towards the upper body (Figure 5.6). The left arm was flexed at the elbow and the wrist was flexed under the chin. The right arm was extended at the elbow. The skeleton had survived but the bone was very friable and flaky. Only three upper deciduous tooth buds survived and they were unerupted. There was no evidence of pathology.

5.4.2. Burial 3b (Context No. 10016)

Burial 3b (Figure 5.7) was an infant burial, found directly underneath Burial 3a (also an infant). There was no soil between the two coffins, so it is possible that the two were interred at the same time.

Burial 3b was a 2 to 3 year old infant interred in a small fabric-wrapped coffin of a miniature single-break form. It was 36 inches long and 12 inches wide (900mm by

300mm), larger than the 3a coffin, suggesting that Burial 3b was very slightly older and taller than Burial 3a. The lid was trimmed in narrow lead/tin embossed metal ribbon, laid around the edges, across at the head and feet, and crossed over the chest area.

Tree roots had destroyed the entire skeleton and only the developing tooth crowns survived.

5.5. Burial 4 (Context No. 10018)

Burial 4 (Figure 5.8) was located in the area outside the fenced cemetery, and the grave shaft had been cut through by an old offal pit. Some coffin fragments were found in the offal pit fill, but fortunately the burial itself had not been disturbed. The burial was identified as Dr. Gustavus Weber by the (just) legible iron coffin plate on the lid of the coffin (see the discussion of coffin furniture below). He died aged 41. His late wife, Flora, was interred in Burial 6 (described below).

Dr. Weber's coffin was of the standard single break pattern, made from kauri boards nailed together. It was 6 feet long, 20.5 inches across the shoulders and approximately 8 inches deep. It was covered in a black woollen fabric with a raised nap that had been tacked on. An embossed lead/tin strip (1.5 inches wide) was tacked around the lid and on the coffin sides. Pressed iron coffin plates were fixed to the lid of the coffin at the head and chest. Plain cast iron coffin handles were fixed to the sides of the coffin.

The skeleton of Dr Weber consisted of a partial cranium (the facial bones did not survive) and some upper and lower limb bones. Taphonomic processes rendered most of skeleton unobservable for pathology. From field measurements of his femur and fibula his stature was 173.35 cm ± 3.62 cm. The left mandible and right anterior mandible were present in addition to two loose teeth from the right side of the mandible. He had lost two teeth in his lower jaw antemortem and had a cavity in his left premolar and a gold filling in his left second molar. He had pipe facets on both sides of his mouth and had periodontal disease. His left second molar had extreme taurodontism, a developmental defect that causes an enlargement of the pupal chamber in the apical/occlusal aspect and is

Fig. 5.8. Burial 4 (Dr. Weber, to the right) and Burial 6 (Flora Weber, to the left).

thought to be a genetically determined trait (Jafarzadeh et al. 2008). He also had evidence of childhood growth disruption (LEH) in one of his teeth.

5.6. Burial 5 (Context No. 10012)

Burial 5 (Figure 5.9) was of a child of 7 to 12 years old, of unknown identity. The burial was located in the area outside the modern cemetery fence. The wooden coffin was of standard single-break shape, 5 feet 8 inches long and 20 inches wide across the shoulders (1.73m by 500mm). The coffin was fabric-covered and was decorated with embossed lead/tin ribbon along the lid edges and across the lid at 1/3 and 2/3 of its length. There was an iron shield-shaped coffin plate in the centre of the coffin (over the abdomen), but there was no legible writing. Rust stains indicated that there may also have been head and foot plates.

The bottom of the grave was slightly curved (the head and feet were higher than the middle), and the coffin and skeleton had sunk into this curve. The curve was probably due to the grave diggers neglecting to fully dig into the ends in the somewhat small grave cut.

Fig. 5.9. Burial 5 after the coffin lid was removed (but with the coffin plate over the abdomen still in place)

The skeleton was poorly preserved, and was not lifted. The outlines of the limb bones were present *in situ* but the bone tissue was extremely friable and lacking in mineral component. Removal of the bones would have destroyed what was remaining. For this reason only analytical samples were taken, consisting of the teeth that were present and bone samples. As the burial was not lifted, a burial service was held on 7 December when the grave was refilled.

5.7. Burial 6 (Context No. 10016)

Burial 6 (Figure 5.10) was located in the area outside the modern cemetery fence, and was below the water table. The burial was close to and in the same line of interments as Burial 4 (Dr. Weber), and the legible coffin plate confirmed that the individual was Flora Weber, Dr Weber's wife. She died in childbirth in 1874 at the age of 36, predeceasing Dr. Weber by six months.

Flora Weber's coffin was of the standard single break pattern, made from kauri boards nailed together. It was 6 feet long, 19.5 inches across the shoulders and approximately 11 inches deep (1.8m long, 500mm wide and 280mm deep). It was covered in a black fabric with a raised nap. Embossed lead/tin ribbon (1.5 inches wide) was tacked around the lid and on the coffin sides. This had

Fig. 5.10. Burial 6, Flora Weber, with the coffin outline and coffin plate exposed.

a double row of oval motifs. A pressed iron coffin plate was fixed to the lid of the coffin over the chest, with gold painted legend that read 'Flora C. Weber, Aged 36 years.'

It is notable that Flora's and Gustavus' burials shared a number of similarities, other than simply the common employment of black-fabric covered wooden coffins with embossed strip embellishments and named coffin plates. Both coffins were made from kauri, which is a North Island timber although it would have been commonly available due to its widespread use in building construction. Both coffins were also covered in a black fabric with a raised nap; smooth black fabric was more commonly found in the St. John's burials. The embossed metal strips on the coffins were of the same width, but different patterns. It is likely that the same undertaker was employed for both funerals, and treated both in the same manner.

The skeleton of Flora Weber was near complete and well preserved. The joints, muscle attachments and bone surfaces were all mostly observable. Her stature was estimated from her femur to be 157.84 cm ± 3.72 cm. There was no evidence of degenerative joint disease in the limbs. The muscle attachments of her upper limbs were extremely well developed. The only evidence of skeletal pathology was new bone formation in her left maxillary sinus.

Flora Weber had a complete mandible and part left upper jaw. Most of her teeth were present. She had wear patterns on a number of her anterior maxillary and mandibular teeth that suggested extramasticatory use of the teeth, likely for pipe smoking on both sides of the mouth. She had cavities in two of her teeth and an amalgam filling in her lower left first molar. She had lost five of her molars prior to death, had mild calculus and periodontal disease. LEH was present on one of her canines.

5.8. Burial 7 (Context No. 10014)

Burial 7 (Figure 5.11) was an old adult of unknown identity, located in the area outside the modern cemetery fence. The burial was in a wooden coffin of standard single-break pattern, 6 feet 4 inches long and 21 inches across the shoulders (1.93m by 530mm). The coffin was covered in a fine black fabric that was poorly preserved. It was notable for having the most elaborate set of coffin plates found during the 2016 excavation. The embossed iron plates stretched the whole length of the top of the coffin. Unfortunately, no legible inscriptions could be seen. The coffin was also fitted with ornate cast iron handles.

The skeleton was partially intact, but where it had been covered by the iron coffin plates it was very poorly preserved. The outlines of the limb bones were present *in situ* but the bone tissue was extremely friable and lacking in mineral component. Removal of the bones would have destroyed what was remaining. For this reason, it was decided to leave most of the skeleton in situ and lift only the cranium. The upper jaw was partially preserved and

Fig. 5.11. Full length view of Burial 7, with the coffin plates along the top of the coffin exposed.

was edentulous (the teeth had been lost during life). At the position of one of the central incisors there was evidence of infection at the base of the tooth root.

5.9. Burial 8 (Context No. 10058)

Burial 8 (Figure 5.12) was an 18 month old infant of unknown identity found outside the modern cemetery fence, near the end of the old gravel path. The small grave cut (3 feet 10 inches by 14 inches, 1.18m by 360mm) contained a small coffin (3 feet 2 inches by 11 inches, 970mm by 280mm) of single-break form. The coffin was covered in black fabric, and had small plain iron handles.

There was minimal preservation of the postcranial skeleton, and only deciduous teeth remained. Of the teeth present, the two upper central incisors had evidence of slight attrition indicating the infant had been eating solid foods for some time prior to death. Incremental carbon and nitrogen isotope analysis of the tooth dentine show

Fig. 5.12. Burial 8. The outline of the coffin was clear, but the human remains were poorly preserved. The legs of the infant can be seen to the left of centre. The scale is 0.5m long.

that the weaning period for this young child had begun around 6 months of age and ceased just prior to death at 17 months old. A foetal sized portion of a cranial bone was found within the coffin of Burial 8, raising the possibility that this was a double burial that also included a prenatal infant. The teeth of Burial 8 were lifted but other skeletal remains were left in place and, a burial service was held on 15 December when the grave was refilled.

5.10. Burial 9 (Context No. 10015)

Burial 9 (Figure 5.13) was that of Robert Rowley Thomson (or Thompson), aged 47 who died in 1877. He was identified from the preserved inscription on the coffin plate over the chest of the coffin that read 'Robt. R. Thompson, Aged 47 years' (Figure 27). There were also head and foot plates (an angel and a vase respectively, the latter damaged by tree roots). The coffin was covered in black fabric, with embossed lead/tin strips around the edges (on the sides as well as top) and plain cast iron coffin handles. Despite the reasonable preservation of the coffin plates, the coffin itself was poorly preserved, and no timber samples could be obtained for timber identification. The coffin was approximately 6 feet 6 inches (2m) long and 1 foot 9 inches (540mm) wide across the shoulders, and constructed from heavy timbers (3/4 inch thick lid).

Some small fragments of clothing fabric were found when wet sieving the grave contents, and these are discussed in more detail below.

The human remains were also very poorly preserved, and no skeletal or dental material survived. A burial service was accordingly held on 13 December when the grave was refilled.

5.11. Burial 10 (Context No. 10028)

Burial 10 (Figure 5.14) was an old female of unknown identity, located outside the modern cemetery fence. The coffin was of the standard single break pattern but it was

Fig. 5.13. Robert Rowley Thompson's (Burial 9) head and chest plates.

of notably robust construction, and was different to the other coffins examined in several details. It was made from dressed rimu planks that were nominally 1 inch (25mm) thick (most other adult coffins were about ¾ inch (19mm) thick), and while it was not particularly long at 6 feet (1.83m), at 26 inches (660mm) wide it was the widest coffin investigated. In common with the other burials the coffin was covered in black fabric, but the decorative strip was not bright lead/tin (as on other coffins), but rather a 3 inch (76mm) wide black enamelled embossed strip with a recurring star and cursive pattern. This was the only example of this design found. The coffin was also fitted with ornate cast iron handles with a face cast into a roundel in each one, which again was only found on this burial. There was an extra handle at the head of the coffin. There were no coffin plates.

Overall the impression is that this coffin was probably more subdued than other coffins due to the use of black rather than silver trim strip, but it was one of the most expensive coffins examined, with heavier dressed timbers and ornate cast handles. Only the handles of Burials 7 and 29 were comparably ornate, but Burial 10 differed from these in not having any coffin plates, which is unusual given the obvious expense of the rest of the coffin furniture.

The skeleton was generally well preserved. The cranium was present but the maxillae did not survive. Most joint surfaces were observable and in the major limb joints there were no degenerative changes present. Her stature was estimated from her femora to be 157.96cm ± 3.72cm. The cortices of all her limb bones were very thin and the bones generally light in weight. The shafts of her metatarsals were extremely thin and tapered at the distal ends. She may also have suffered from hallux valgus which is a constriction of the big toes from wearing tight poorly fitting shoes. The form of the cranial vault was unusual

Fig. 5.14. Burial 10. The scale is 0.5m long.

in shape. The frontal bone was very short and vertical, the metopic suture was retained and the superior surface of the vault was unusually flattened. The internal sinuses of the sphenoid were enlarged. The mandible of this individual showed most of the posterior teeth had been lost in life. It appears that some of the anterior mandibular teeth were intact at the time of death but the post-mortem damage made it impossible to determine exactly how many. She also suffered from severe periodontal disease.

5.12. Burial 11 (Context No. 10029)

Burial 11 (Figure 5.15) was an adult (middle aged) male found outside the modern cemetery fence, in the main row of burials along the gravel path. From the injuries present it is suspected that it is Joseph Higgins who died in a mining accident in 1877 aged 37. It was the only burial investigated in the cemetery that had evidence of an individual fence around the grave: four post holes with the butts of square posts were found around the grave cut. Similar examples can be seen surviving in numerous historic cemeteries in Central Otago (where timber survives well). The butts were very decayed, and were identified as either rimu or totara (the latter seems more likely given the need for durable posts).

The burial was in a timber coffin of standard single-break pattern, 6 feet 4 inches (1.93m) long and 20.5 inches (520mm) wide at the shoulders. The sides had been made from single boards that had been curved at the shoulders: the vertical kerf cuts could still be seen on the inside surface. One coffin floor plank appeared to have paint on it, possibly suggesting that second-hand timbers were used in the coffin construction. The coffin was covered with black fabric and trimmed with embossed lead/tin strips, and a sheet iron coffin plate was present but was too corroded to read. Plain iron coffin handles were fitted.

The skeleton was well-preserved. The skull, including the face and mandible, was near complete and was the best preserved in the cemetery sample. Most of the joint surfaces were observable but many of the bone surfaces were covered in what may have been paint that had originally been applied to the coffin and had coated the bones as the coffin timber decayed away. His stature was estimated from his femur to be 169.83 cm ± 3.94 cm.

Multiple traumatic injuries that had healed (antemortem) and that occurred around death and were unhealed (perimortem) were present. A perimortem cranial injury was present on the right temporal squamous portion, extending into the greater wing of the sphenoid. In the left upper limb there was a depressed linear defect in the apex of the trochlear space of the humerus and posterior trochlear surface. Radiography revealed a well remodelled fracture of the capitulum beginning at the point of the defect. The left humerus was 8mm shorter than the right. The distal thumb phalanx of the left hand was shortened and flattened. One of the carpal bones of the hand, the lunate, was also shortened. Both of these bone changes are

Fig. 5.15. Burial 11. The scale is 0.5m long.

probably the result of healed fractures. In the left femur there was a perimortem comminuted (broken into several pieces) fracture of distal third of the shaft. Sharp force perimortem trauma of one lower right rib and a healed fracture of another right rib from the mid thorax region were also present. A number of erosive lesions associated with joints were also identified.

Most of the dentition of this individual was present and *in situ*. He had lost his right lower first molar during life. There was crowding of the anterior maxillary teeth and the lateral maxillary incisors were rotated and overlapped with the central incisors. There was also crowding of the anterior mandibular teeth with the mandibular canines rotated labially to allow space for the mandibular incisors. Tooth cavities (n=11) were widespread throughout the dentition and were mostly of the massive type (n=7), to the extent that a number of these teeth had the crown destroyed and only the root remained. A massive alveolar lesion was observable on the posterior right maxilla likely due to infection spreading from the exposure of the pulp cavity from carious destruction. Pipe facets were observed on the incisors and canines of the maxilla and mandible on both sides of the mouth. He also had severe periodontal

disease. There were numerous LEH present on all the anterior mandibular teeth (incisors and canines) and a number of the anterior maxillary teeth, with many in the upper third of the crown, correlating with the youngest phase of tooth development.

The observable unhealed injuries of his skull match closely those described that caused the death of Joseph Higgins, who was killed in a rock fall at the Canada Reef gold workings on 8 November 1877 (*Bruce Herald* 13 November 1877).

5.13. Burial 12

This was the grave of Henry Pim. The broken gravestone was found during topsoil stripping; one section was just below the surface, and one section was visible on the ground before excavation. Both sections were displaced, but the original stone setting was found at the head of the grave cut, so the grave was confidently located. The grave was in one of the main rows of burials, between Burials 11 and 13.

As already discussed, the formal permissions were explicitly for unmarked graves, so once the grave marker was found this grave was not investigated further. However, Henry Pim is discussed further below in the consideration of the social context of the cemetery.

5.14. Burial 13 (Context No. 10026)

Burial 13 (Figure 5.16) was an adult (possibly middle aged) male burial in a standard pattern single break wooden coffin. The coffin was 6 feet 2 inches (1.88m) long, 22 inches (560mm) wide across the shoulders and 11 inches deep. It was covered in black fabric, and had a large iron sheet coffin plate over the chest area, but no writing was legible. There were the impressions of plant stalks across this plate (the impressions preserved in the rust): these were possibly the stalks of flowers laid across the coffin. Despite the presence of a large ornate coffin plate, the coffin did not have any embossed metallic ribbon decoration nor any iron handles. It is possible that the coffin had rope handles that had left no trace. Three ½ inch diameter fabric-covered buttons were found with the burial, on the chest area.

The individual was supine, elbows flexed with his hands placed over his pelvis. The skeleton was complete and was in good condition. Most of the bones and the teeth were covered with a yellowish calcified concretion. The cranium was complete and the upper and lower jaws were partially present. His stature was estimated from his femora to be 173.64cm ± 3.94cm.

There were bowing deformities in the lower limb bones suggestive of trauma, but difficult to differentiate from taphonomic processes in the burial environment. Three antemortem rib fractures were present, one on the right and two on the left side. Where the joint surfaces were

Fig. 5.16. Burial 13 upper body, showing the large coffin plate over the chest area.

Fig. 5.17. Burial 14, showing the mass of tree roots where the coffin once existed.

Fig. 5.18. Burial 15. The rectangular outline of the grave cut was very clear in the clay, but the coffin and individual were poorly preserved.

observable (either complete or in part) there were no degenerative changes present (i.e. the distal right radius, elbows, hips and most of the axial fragments). He also had a number of erosive joint lesions of the upper limb. A small piece of the maxilla was intact, but no associated teeth were present. The right side of the mandible and anterior left side of the mandible were also intact but only five teeth were present. He had four teeth, with all molars lost antemortem in right lower jaw. A pipe wear facet was present on his lower right canine that also had an LEH lesion. He also had widespread periodontal disease.

5.15. Burial 14 (Context No. 10027)

Burial 14 (Figure 5.17) was an infant based on the size of the coffin, but all that remained of both the coffin and the burial itself was a mass of roots within the coffin void. The coffin was probably about 20 inches (0.5m) long.

5.16. Burial 15 (Context No. 10042)

Burial 15 (Figure 5.18) was an infant burial in a clay matrix, and the backfill was waterlogged clay. The small grave cut (3 feet 5 inches by 1 foot 5 inches, 1.05m by 0.44m) contained the shadow of a small coffin, but the timber was completely rotten and no clear outline could be determined, other than by the location of some very corroded nails. Fabric found within the coffin shadow

appeared to be a shroud or body wrapping (possibly the baby's blanket) rather than a coffin cover.

Some fragments of bone were present, but not enough for any analysis.

5.17. Burial 16 (Context No. 10043)

Burial 16 (Figure 5.19) was a young child (18 months to 2.5 years old) found within the fenced area, in the main row of burials along the gravel path. The coffin was of the standard single-break pattern, and was small, measuring 3 feet long by 11 inches across the shoulders (920mm by 280mm). It was covered in black fabric and the lid and sides were trimmed with 7/16 inch (11mm) wide lead/tin strip, and the fabric had been preserved where these strips ran, showing that they had been crossed across the chest. There were no coffin handles.

The skeleton of this young child did not survive, however, teeth, hair and finger and toes nails were present (Figure 5.20). The hair was at least 15 cm long and plaited, suggesting this was a female. This young child had a cavity in one of their upper deciduous molars and slight

Fig. 5.19. Burial 16 grave cut and coffin. The coffin fabric was preserved in a cross across the chest, showing where lead/tin embossed metal strip had been placed. The scale is 0.5m long.

Fig. 5.20. Burial 16, showing the preserved hair and teeth of the young child.

Fig. 5.21. Burial 17, with the shadow outline of the coffin left standing, but nothing was found of the individual.

5.19. Burial 18 (Context No. 10044)

Burial 18 (Figure 5.22) was a small child (approximately 1 to 2 years old), cut into clay and with wet clay fill. The grave cut measured 3 feet 6 inches by 1 foot 5 inches (1.07m by 0.43m), with the coffin a very close fit within the grave at 3 feet 3 inches long and 11 inches wide (1m by 0.28m). The coffin was of a miniature single break pattern, and was constructed of ¾ inch (19mm) thick timbers, heavier than used on any other infant burials in the cemetery. The coffin was covered in a very degraded lightweight fabric, and had been trimmed with 1 inch (25mm) wide embossed lead/tin ribbon (which was also poorly preserved). There were no handles. Within the coffin there were plant fibres under the head of the individual.

The skeleton of this young child did not survive, however, teeth and hair were present. The hair was 40mm long. The teeth were not very well preserved but the lower incisors had slight wear on them indicating consumption of solid foods sometime before death. Incremental isotope analysis of the hair suggests they were fully weaned by 14 months

wear on their lower incisors indicating consumption of solid foods sometime prior to death. Incremental isotope analysis of the hair suggests they were fully weaned by 20 months of age. The cavity suggests the foods used to supplement their diet during weaning included starchy or sugary substances.

5.18. Burial 17 (Context No. 10041)

Burial 17 (Figure 5.21) was an infant burial in a very wet clay matrix. The coffin was rectangular and measured 17 inches by 11 inches (430mm by 280mm), and approximately 6 inches (135mm) deep. It was secured with iron nails, and had no fabric cover. The timber was very poorly preserved, and no sample could be taken.

Nothing remained of the skeleton.

Fig. 5.22. Burial 18. The coffin wood was reasonably well preserved, but the human remains consisted only of hair and teeth. The scale is 0.5m long.

of age. There was also a spike in nitrogen values noted within the last 3 months of their life that may indicate severe stress during this period.

5.20. Burial 19 (Context No. 10045)

Burial 19 (Figure 5.23) was a young child approximately 1 year old (within a range of 9 to 18 months), and was buried with the head to the north. This was the only burial so aligned: all of the other burials that were investigated in the cemetery were the other way around.

Burial 19 was in the main row of burials along the gravel path, inside the fenced cemetery area. The small coffin was a standard single break form, but was only 3 feet long and 9 ¼ inches wide (910mm by 235mm). It was fabric covered, but the fabric was in very poor condition. There was a faint shadow over the chest that may have been the remains of a coffin plate, but it was too poorly preserved to tell.

The skeleton of this young child did not survive, but teeth and hair were present. Two of the canine teeth had a defect in the enamel (LHPC) that indicates a period of stress at around 6 months of age. This defect has been associated with poor maternal health (as the deciduous teeth form in utero) and may also represent localised trauma to the mouth from putting hard objects into their mouth, a behaviour that starts around 6 months of age.

The hair was at least 70mm long, and incremental isotope analysis suggests that weaning began around 6 months of age and was complete at the time of death. The timing of the initiation of weaning corresponds with the period of the dental defect development, suggesting a relationship between the two.

Fig. 5.23. Burial 19. The coffin outline was well defined, but the human remains consisted only of hair and teeth.

5.21. Burials 20a (Context No. 10046) and 20b (Context No. 10059)

Burials 20a and 20b were of two young children (an infant less than 1 year old and a young child of about 3 years) in the same grave, located in the main burial row beside the gravel path, within the fenced area of the cemetery. They were both in coffins, buried one on top of the other. The upper coffin contained Burial 20a, the lower coffin contained Burial 20b. The timber of both coffins was poorly preserved, and the two had collapsed down together.

It is likely that these were the Caudle sisters. In the historical record there is an account of two sisters who died on the same day of whooping cough (Finlay et al 2015: 28). Catherine Caudle was reported as being approximately 1 year old when she died, and Lucy Caudle was reported as being 3 years and 4 months old. The age estimates from dental development roughly correlate with the ages of the Caudle sisters and the long hair (9-10 cm long) of B20B indicates this was probably a female. We do not have the death certificates for these children to assess the length of their illness.

5.21.1. Burial 20a (Context No. 10046)

Burial 20a (Figure 5.24) was an infant of approximately 14months of age (estimated range 1.3-1.6 years). The small coffin was of the single break form, and was 2 feet 8 inches long and 10 inches wide (810mm by 250mm). It was covered in black fabric, and there was no evidence of other decorative treatment.

The skeleton of this young child did not survive, but teeth and hair were present. The hair was at least 30mm long. The teeth were not very well preserved but the lower incisors had moderate wear on them indicating consumption of solid foods sometime before death. There were not enough increments of the hair to allow for estimating weaning time using isotopic analysis. Evidence of stress in utero is present in the form of enamel defects on one of the lower canines. These developed at around 4.5 and 10.5 months of age.

Fig. 5.24. The Burial 20a coffin sitting within the Burial 20b coffin, as a result of the two collapsing together. The scale is 0.5m long.

5.21.2. Burial 20b (Context No. 10059)

Burial 20b (Figure 5.25) was a young child of around 3 years old (age range 2.5-4.5 years). The small coffin was of the single break form, and was 3 feet 6 inches long and 13 inches wide (1.07m by 330mm), and approximately 7 inches (180mm) deep. It was covered in black fabric, and there was no evidence of other decorative treatment.

No skeletal material remained, and only the teeth and a full head of hair survived. The hair was at least 90-100mm

Fig. 5.25. The Burial 20b coffin after Burial 20a had been removed.

long. On cleaning the hair in the laboratory it was observed that it had been plaited. Incremental isotope analysis of 70mm of the hair indicates this child was weaned before 2.5 years of age. There were multiple carious cavities in their upper and lower deciduous teeth suggesting exposure to a starchy and/or sugary diet.

5.22. Burial 21 (Context No. 10047)

Burial 21 (Figure 5.26) was William Toogood, a 42 year old male who was identified from the legible coffin plate. The interment was in the main row of burials along the gravel path. The wooden coffin was of the traditional single break style, 6 feet 5 inches (1.95m) long. The coffin was wrapped in a black fabric, with embossed lead/tin alloy decorative metal strips around the edges of the lid and coffin sides. There were six plain cast iron coffin handles. What was notable was the presence of a legible coffin plate and evidence of a painted design on the coffin top fabric. The coffin plate identified the individual but unfortunately the painted design was too degraded to identify any detail, other than it has been extensive and ornate.

The coffin had evidently retained its integrity for some time after burial, as it had filled with water and allowed the skeleton to become disarticulated and move around after the connective tissue had decayed. Only later did the top collapse, stopping any further movement. The skeleton was very well-preserved and near complete, but as a result of this post-burial movement the body was largely disarticulated and some bones were fragmented.

His stature was estimated from his femur as 163.9 ± 3.87cm. There was skeletal evidence of tuberculosis in his hips and cranium. There was a partial maxilla and complete mandible present, and he had lost six of his teeth antemortem. There were pipe wear facets on the right maxillary and mandibular lateral incisors and right mandibular canine. He had five cavities, two of which destroyed the entire tooth crown. He also suffered from periodontal disease. There were a number of LEH defects on six teeth and four of these teeth had two or three LEH per tooth indicating a series of stressful physiological events during childhood.

A detailed integrated case study of this individual's life history has been published (Snoddy et al. 2020). His history is considered in more detail below.

Fig. 5.26. Burial 21, showing how the skeleton was disarticulated. The scale is 0.5m long.

5.23. Burial 22 (Context No. 10048)

Burial 22 (Figure 5.27) was an adult (possibly female) within a large grave cut into clay that was initially thought likely to contain a multiple burial, but was found to contain only one fairly small coffin. The size of the cut was 7 feet 2 inches by 3 feet (2.2m by 0.9m), but the coffin only measured 5 feet 9 inches long by 20 inches wide across the shoulders (1.75m by 510mm). It was of the usual single-break form, but the timber was very degraded. There was no discernable coffin plate but there was a rectangular shadow at an angle across the chest, measuring 12 inches by 4 inches (300mm x 100mm).

Fig. 5.27. Burial 22. The outline of the skeleton was reasonably clear, but the bones were very poorly preserved.

The skeleton was poorly preserved. The outlines of the limb bones were present *in situ* but the bone tissue was extremely friable and lacking in mineral component. Removal of the bones would have destroyed what was remaining, and only small analytical samples were taken. As the body was left in place a burial service was held on 14 December when the grave was refilled.

5.24. Burial 23 (Context No. 10049)

Burial 23 (Figure 5.28) was an adult (possibly female) and was in the main line of burials along the gravel path, inside the fenced area of the cemetery. The coffin was of the standard single break form, and was quite large at 6 feet 4 inches long and 23 inches wide (1.93m by 590mm) and 10 inches (250mm) deep. It was covered with black fabric and the lid was trimmed with 1 inch (25mm) wide embossed lead/tin strip, while the sides were trimmed with 2 inch (50mm) wide strip. The coffin had plain cast iron handles, and in addition to the usual three on each side there were also handles at the head and feet (eight handles in total). The large coffin and large number of handles might suggest that the individual was large and heavy.

The skeletal tissue was in very poor condition. There was some hair preserved and a complete calcified brain was present. The outlines of the limb bones were present *in situ* but the bone tissue was extremely friable and lacking in mineral component. Removal of the bones would have destroyed what was remaining. For this reason, it was decided to leave most of the skeleton *in situ* and lift only the mandible, a sample of hair and the complete brain.

5.25. Burial 24

The Burial 24 grave cut was exposed during topsoil stripping, but the grave was not further investigated.

5.26. Burial 25

The Burial 25 grave cut was exposed during topsoil stripping, but the grave was not further investigated.

5.27. Burial 26

The Burial 26 grave cut was exposed during topsoil stripping, but the grave was not further investigated.

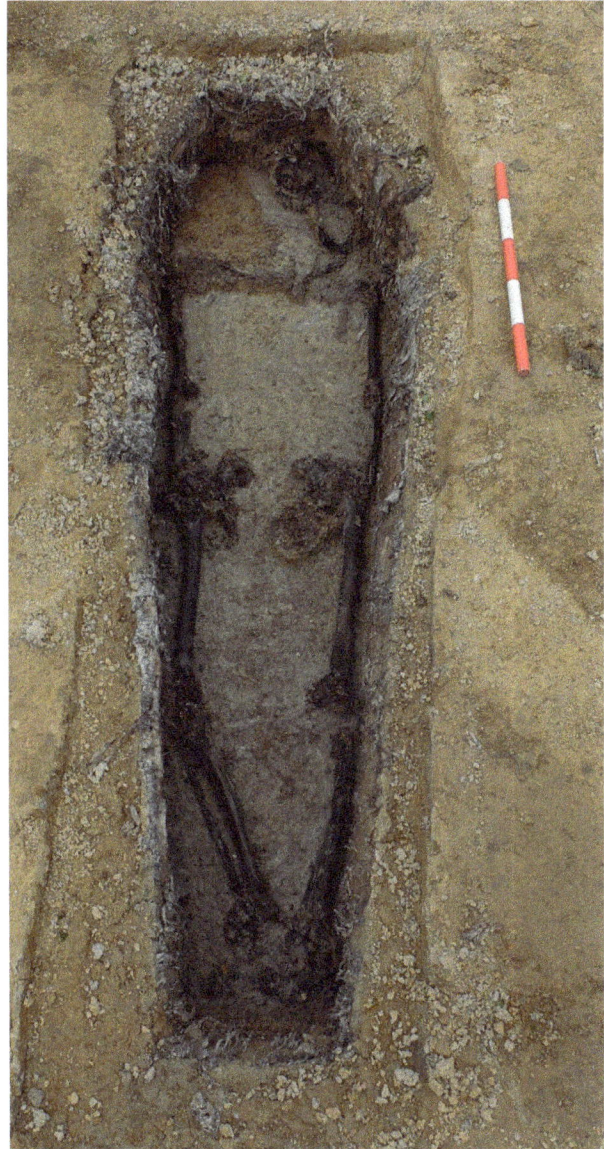

Fig. 5.28. Burial 23, showing the intact limbs, but the torso was very poorly preserved. The scale is 0.5m long.

5.28. Burial 27 (Context No. 10053)

Burial 27 (Figure 5.29) was an infant (estimated at 1.3 to 1.5 years old) whose grave was cut into clay, with a wet clay backfill. The small grave (4 feet 3 inches by 1 foot 9 inches, 1.3m by 0.54m) contained a small wooden coffin. This coffin was a miniature single break pattern, 32 inches long and 10 inches across the shoulders (810mm by 250mm). It had 1 inch (25mm) wide lead/tin embossed strip decoration around the top of the lid and the sides, and was fitted with miniature cast iron handles. It was an almost exact copy of the larger adult burial coffins, apart from the absence of a coffin plate.

The skeleton was poorly preserved, and only the teeth and hair remained. Evidence of dental enamel defects indicates that there were multiple episodes of *in utero* stress from around 12 foetal weeks to birth. One of these defects was a carious lesion that forms at the site of

Fig. 5.29. Burial 27, showing the wet clay into which the grave was dug. The scale is 0.5m long.

poorly mineralised enamel on the upper central incisors, known as 'circular caries'. This infant also had u-shaped notches at the occlusal part of the lower central incisors. These defects would have formed between 12 and 30 foetal weeks and may have been caused by vitamin D deficiency of the mother during the baby's development. There was no information on the weaning time for this individual.

5.29. Burial 28 (Context No. 10056)

Burial 28 (Figure 5.30) was a perinatal infant (estimated 38 foetal weeks to 3 months old) in the main row of burials along the gravel path, but located outside the present fenced area of the cemetery. The small coffin was trapezoidal in shape, 2 feet 4 inches long, 8 inches across the head and 6 inches across the feet, and 5 ½ inches deep (710mm by 200mm by 150mm, by 140mm deep). It was covered in black fabric, and trimmed with 7/16 inch (11mm) wide embossed lead/tin strip. The remains of an iron star was on the centre of the lid.

Skeletal and dental material survived, but the bone tissue was very friable and delicate and could not be lifted intact. Age estimation was based on the dental and cranial development.

Fig. 5.30. Burial 28, with the infant skeleton partially intact within the wooden coffin.

5.30. Burial 29 (Context No. 10057)

Burial 29 (Figure 5.31) was a young to middle aged (20-34 years) female whose grave was located outside of the current fenced cemetery area. The wooden coffin was of the standard single break pattern, 6 feet 3 inches long, 21 inches across the shoulders and 10 ½ inches deep (1.9m by 530mm by 270mm). It was made from 7/8 inch (22mm) thick timbers, but these were very decayed and were not identified. The coffin was covered with black fabric that had been fixed using iron tacks. A decorative silver-coloured embossed strip (lead/tin alloy) was tacked around the coffin lid. This was poorly preserved, but appeared to have a double row of curved motifs. A pressed iron coffin plate was present on the top of the lid, but this was very corroded and no writing was discernable. The plate was large, and based on other examples probably had a central shield (with the name and age of the deceased) bounded on all four sides by religious motifs (such as angels). The coffin was fitted with eight V-shaped cast iron handles.

5.30. Burial 29, showing the well-preserved skeleton. The scale is 0.5m long.

Burial 29 is the most enigmatic of the well-preserved adults from this site. Her biological history has been published in an integrated case study (Snoddy et al. 2021). The cranium is complete but the facial region did not survive well. Her stature was estimated from her fibula to be 174.17cm $\pm$ 3.57 cm. However, it should be mentioned that the stature estimates from her lower limbs differed by more than two standard deviations to those from her upper limbs which yielded stature estimates closer to 164cm.

A possible perimortem sharp force injury was observed in the anterior sternum *in situ*. This individual also had lateral bowing deformities of the humeri, ribs, and left femur. The left rib shafts were thickened considerably and ribs 3-8 had abnormal flattening and superior curvature of the shafts and a deep costal groove. The costal cartilage of the lower right ribs was calcified. This woman was also unusually tall based on her lower limb stature estimates, but with large discrepancies between the upper and lower limbs (see above). Several of the entheses on the left side, including the insertion for the iliofemoral and costoclavicular ligaments, were unusually pronounced. She also had marginal erosive lesions in the metacarpals of both hands and feet.

The dentition of this individual included a complete mandible and three loose maxillary teeth. The left and right mandibular molars were lost antemortem. This individual would have had a diastema (gap) in between her central mandibular incisors. She had a cavity in one of her teeth and periodontal disease. Her right upper first premolar was unusually large and she had a deformed permanent molar (2nd right maxillary) or possibly a malformed supplementary supernumerary molar.

6

The Human Remains

Twenty-five graves were investigated, with the remains of 27 individuals found due to two of the graves being double burials (3a, 3b and 20a, 20b). The preservation of the skeletons was highly variable, ranging from no bone in most of the subadult graves to excellent preservation in a small number of adults. Many of the subadults were represented by dentition only and some adult bone was extremely soft, to the point where in some cases only a 'shadow' of bone remained. This has presented challenges in not only determining individual details, but also the overall health of the population represented. In many cases recording of the human remains had to be carried out *in situ*, as the bones were too fragile to lift (such as the measurement of femora to determine stature), and this has inevitably affected the accuracy of some age, sex and stature estimations. The skeletal preservation of the subadults in particular was minimal, so any information on their health and diet can only be gleaned from their teeth, thereby negating any assessment of skeletal growth and health in most subadults. Nevertheless, a great deal of information about this population could be determined, particularly through the chemical analyses of diet and health. The following information is summarised from a number of papers that have been published regarding osteological and historical epidemiology and dietary isotope analysis carried out on these individuals (Buckley et al 2020; King et al 2021a; King et al 2021b; King et al 2020; Snoddy et al 2020; Snoddy et al 2021). In these publications and the summaries presented here, we have focussed on gleaning as much information as possible on the lived experiences of individuals, through integrated case-studies of the life course. Analyses of this detail are rarely carried in large scale population-based analyses of cemeteries from any period.

6.1. Age and Sex Estimations

The sample of individuals excavated in 2016 range in age from preterm infants to old aged adults. A multifactorial approach was used in the estimation of the age at death of adults. Standard measures used were observations of late fusing epiphyses (sternal clavicle and sacrum), pubic symphysis and auricular morphology and dental wear seriation (Buikstra and Ubelaker 1994). Adults were classified in relative age groups of young, middle and old aged (Buikstra and Ubelaker 1994). The estimation of sex for adults was based on standard morphological observations of the pelvis and cranium (Buikstra and Ubelaker 1994). Preference was given to pelvis morphology as this is a more accurate reflection of sex. Ten adults were excavated, four males, five females and one (Burial 7) for which we could not assign sex. Most of the adults were either middle aged or old at the

time of death. Interpretations of the skeletal pathology observed in the seven well-preserved adults are discussed together in an attempt to place these individuals within the context of the wider community and begin to assess 'population' health of these early settlers. The other three adults were either not excavated or had extremely poor skeletal preservation, precluding an assessment of health. The profiles of all adults, including skeletal health and pathology observations are briefly presented in Table 6.1.

Infants and children (subadults) are defined throughout as those under 15 years of age at death. This definition is based on purely biological factors, where skeletal linear growth is usually completed around this age (Scheuer and Black 2000). It is acknowledged however that children and adolescents under this age may have been viewed by the wider society as adults, engaged in wage earning work, and young women could marry as young as 12 years old with the permission of a parent or guardian (Eldred-Grigg 1984: 18; https://teara.govt.nz/en/marriage-and-partnering/page-2).

Age at death of infants and children was estimated using dental formation stages (Moorrees et al. 1963b, a), as dental methods are the most accurate for this age group and in most cases at SJM only dental remains survived. Where skeletal material was present, methods based on skeletal development and estimated size of skeletal elements were also used (Scheuer and Black 2000). Those less than 15 years of age at death constitute 61.5% (n=16/25) of those excavated, and over half of these died before one year of age. Two of the subadult graves were double burials (probably simultaneous interments), each with their own coffin (Burials 3A and 3B and 20A and 20B). Another case of a possible double burial occurred with Burial 8, a 1 to 1.5 year old child, where a foetal cranial bone (petrous portion of temporal) from within the grave was identified in the laboratory.

Three subadults (Burials 14, 15 and 17) were not able to have an age estimation assigned due to poor preservation but the small coffin sizes of these individuals suggest that they were of prenatal-perinatal age. Consideration of the range of coffin dimensions was used to inform all of the age estimations, with infant and child burials in coffins from 2 feet 1 inch (635mm) to 5 feet 8 inches (1.73m) long (the largest being of a child up to 12 years old), and adult coffins from that size up to 6 feet 6 inches (1.98m) long. No attempt was made to sex infants and children due to the lack of sexual dimorphism in the pelvis and skull before puberty. Details of the subadult age estimations and preservation are presented in Table 6.2.

Table 6.1. Details of adults excavated at SJM. B=Burial, A=Age, S=Sex, ID=Identified, Stat=Stature.

B	A	S	ID	Death certificate	Material present	Stat. (cm)	Skeletal pathology	Comments
4	41y	M	yes	Alcoholism, chloroform abuse.	Poorly preserved bones most surface unobservable. Some teeth	169.8	Unobservable	Identified *in situ*.
6	36y	F	yes	Complications of childbirth	Good preservation of complete skeleton. Some damage to cranium.	164.8	Well-developed entheses of upper limb. Maxillary sinusitis	Identified *in situ*. Wife of local doctor.
7	Old	?	no	-	Complete very poorly preserved skeleton. Edentulous maxilla fragment.		Unobservable in postcranial bones. Moderate hyperostosis frontalis interna on left.	Cranium and long bone fragment sampled. Rest reburied (poor preservation)
9	47y	M	Yes	Tuberculosis. *"Pthisis pulmondes"*	No skeletal or dental remains preserved	-	-	Identified *in situ*
10	Old	F	No	-	V. good preservation of bone. Thorax damaged by coffin plate. Edentulous		Thin diaphyseal cortices, light bone. Retention of metopic suture.	
11	Mid	M	Prob	(?) Injuries due to mining accident	Excellent preservation of skeletal and dental. Hair preserved.	168.3	Perimortem and antemortem trauma.	Poss. identification
12	?	M	Yes		Not excavated			Not exc.
13	Mid?	M	No		Good preservation *in situ*. Cranium damaged. Deteriorated during drying.	173.8	Antemortem fractures and enthesopathies. Robust and marked entheses. Most bone surfaces eroded.	
21	42y	M	Yes	Tuberculosis. *"Pneumonic pthisis haemorrhage"*	Well preserved skeletal and dental, but fragmented and disarticulated. Hair and brain tissue.	173.4	Skeletal tuberculosis lesions of hips and cranium (ref).	Identified *in situ*. Labourer. Invalid for 12 months before death.
22	Adult	F?	No		Very poorly preserved skeletal material. Dentition present.	156.9	Unobservable	Not fully exhumed (poor preservation). Bone samples taken.
23	Adult	F?	No		Very poorly preserved skeletal and dental. Hair and complete calcified brain present.	164.3	Unobservable	Not fully exhumed due to poor preservation. Cranium and dentition lifted.
24								Not excavated
25								Not excavated
26								Not excavated
29	Mid	F	No		Well preserved skeletal and dental. Damage to cranium.	177.9	Skeletal dysplasia (bowing of limbs, deformity of ribs). Poss. perimortem sharp force injury to sternum.	

6.2. Stature

The eventual height (stature) attained by an adult is a reflection of a complex interplay between the genetic potential for height and the influence of the environment during growth (Eveleth and Tanner 1990). Therefore, adult stature can be used as a measure of population health. Long bone lengths were all measured *in situ* before being removed from the ground. If intact after lifting the bone was measured again in the laboratory and this was taken as the more accurate measurement, Stature was estimated using standards created from the limb bone measurements of "white" American males and females (Trotter and Gleser 1952; Trotter and Gleser 1958) as these samples are ethnically similar to the European settlers at Milton. Stature was estimated from the lower limb bones where possible as these equations are accompanied by the smallest margin of error.

Average stature in the St. Johns Cemetery sample was 170.2cm (5ft 5in) for males (range 169.63cm-173.64cm and 161.83 cm (5ft 3in) for females (range 157.84cm-163.77cm).

Table 6.2. Details of all subadults excavated at SJM. B=Burial, A=Age, S=Sex, ID=Identified, Stat=Stature.

B	A	Age Range	Aged from	Possible matches	Coffin length (ft in)	Comment
1	4-5y		Dentition	Edwin Butler 6yrs, Elizabeth Cockerill 4yrs, Anna Bella Moore 6 yrs	4' 11"	Dentition only
2	Perinate	Prenatal to perinate (just post birth)	Dentition and cranial dev.	Nanny Bradbury Powley 27 days, John Fyffe 19 days, Baby Mansford stillbirth	2' 4"	Dent. and skeletal material pres. No diaphyseal metric possible
3A	Perinate	34-40 foetal weeks	Dentition, cranial dev. and cranial metrics	Nanny Bradbury Powley 27 days, John Fyffe 19 days, Baby Mansford stillbirth	1' 11"	Double burial (3B). Dent. and skeletal material pres. No diaphyseal metric possible
3B	2.5y	2-3 years	Dev. of perm. tooth crowns	Edward Budgen, 2yrs10mo, Mary Anne Flahive 2yrs, Levi Snow 3yrs	2' 4"	Double burial (3A). Only tooth crowns remain.
5	?7-8y	7-12	Dental dev.	John Edwards 7yrs, Anna Bella Moore 6yrs, Henry Farrell 15 yrs	5' 8"	Coffin may indicate older age. Poorly pres. bone and dentition
8	1.5y	1.5-2 years	Dental dev.	Frederick Clegg 15mo, Mary Anne Flahive 2yrs, George Powley 15mo,	3' 2"	Poor bone pres. No diaphyseal metrics possible. Tiny (7.5mm) pars petrous may indicate 2nd foetal indiv. in coffin
14	?Prenatal-perinatal	-	Coffin size	Baby Mansford stillbirth, John Fyffe 19 days, Nanny Bradbury Powley 27 days	approx 1' 8"	No skeletal or dental material remaining
15	?Prenatal-perinatal	-	Coffin size	Baby Mansford stillbirth, John Fyffe 19 days, Nanny Bradbury Powley 27 days	approx 1' 6"	No skeletal or dental material remaining
16	2y	1.5-2.5 years	Dental dev.	Mary Ann Flahive 2yrs	1' 3"	No bone. Teeth, long plaited hair and finger and toe nails present
17	?Prenatal-perinatal	-	Coffin size	Nanny Bradbury Powley 27 days	1' 5"	No skeletal or dental material remaining
18	1.5y	1-2 years	Dental dev.	Stephen Caudle 1yr, Frederick Clegg 15mo, Mary Ann Flahive 2yrs, George Powley 15mo,	2' 9"	No bone. Teeth and hair present. Tooth shape and size (v. small constricted deciduous crowns) sim. to 20A
19	1.0y	.75 -1.5 years	Dental dev.	Alice May Daniels 9mo, Grace Mathilda Ronaldson 11mo, Bertha Mathilda 9mo	1' 3"	No bone present but teeth and hair (7cm) present
20A	15 months	1.3-1.6 years	Dental dev.	Catherine Caudle. Just over 1 year of age Hist. record of Caudle sisters d. same day (16/6/1873), whooping cough.	2' 8"	Double burial (20B). Teeth and hair only.
20B	3y	2.5-4.5 years	Dental dev.	Lucy Caudle 3 years and 4 months. Hist. record of Caudle sisters d. same day (16/6/1873), whooping cough	3' 6"	Double burial (20A). Teeth and hair only.
27	15m	1.3-1.5 (15-18months)		Frederick Clegg 15mo George Powley 15mo	2' 8"	
28	Perinate	38fwks-3 months old	Skeletal maturation		??	

6.3. Oral Health

The oral health of the people have been published in two papers; Buckley et al. (2020) for the adults and King et al. (2021) for the subadults. There were four middle-aged adult males (B4, B11, B13, B21), two middle aged adult females (B6 and B29) and an individual of unknown age and sex (B23) with preserved dentition. Nine subadults had dentition present. Many of the teeth were brittle with cracked or flaking enamel and blue/black staining, indicating poor preservation in the burial environment. Analysis of the dentition falls into three main categories: developmental anomalies that reflect foetal and childhood health; general dental health during life (which includes caries and periodontal disease); and isotopic analysis of tooth enamel to study diet and individual origins.

All but one of the St John's adults and two of the subadults had linear enamel hypoplasia (LEH), which is a pattern of dental defects indicating disruption of growth during development due to physiological stress. Other types of developmental disruptions present in the teeth were found in two of the infants deciduous or baby teeth. Because the deciduous teeth develop prior to birth, these defects represent physiological stress to the mother while pregnant. All of the adults with appropriate dentition (n=7) from SJM have been isotopically identified as non-local, and thus are likely first-generation colonists to New Zealand (King et al. 2020). As these episodes of stress occurred during childhood, they represent periods of stress at 'home' rather than in New Zealand and suggests that affected individuals were of a working-class background, where disease and dietary deficiencies would have been more prevalent than for more affluent individuals. There are few comparative data from post-medieval period England, however the lower status 'earth cut graves' from St Martins, Birmingham had a similar high LEH prevalence (73.5%) compared with higher status 'vault burials' (47%) (Brickley and Buteux 2006), which supports the interpretation of working-class immigrants buried at St John's.

The overall adult profile is one of poor dental hygiene during life. In all of the adults there were high rates of caries and loss of teeth prior to death, either from massive caries or periodontal disease, or both. The ultimate result of such poor oral health could be the loss of all teeth, and Burial 7 had lost all of their teeth during life. Cavities were also observed in the teeth of some of the young children. All four males with teeth and one middle-aged adult female (B6) had pipe facets in their teeth. These are the distinctive grooves worn in opposing and adjoining teeth as the result of clenching a clay tobacco pipe stem between the teeth. The other female with teeth (B29) did not show evidence of having smoked a pipe.

The oral health of a population can inform on diet, extra-masticatory use of teeth (e.g. pipe smoking), and general health (Hillson 2008). Poor oral health (particularly gum disease) can have severe systemic health consequences (Beck et al. 2000). The poor oral health of the adults from SJM is relatively typical of the time period, with high rates of tooth loss during life as a result of tooth decay and periodontal disease. This pattern fits well with the description of British populations by Roberts and Cox (2003: 324): *"At the outbreak of the First World War many of the working classes still had appalling dental health reflecting a soft cariogenic diet, a lack of oral hygiene and inadequate dental treatment"*.

Two individuals at St. John's Cemetery did have evidence of dental intervention. Gustavus Weber (Burial 4) had a gold filling and his wife Flora Weber (Burial 6) had an amalgam (mercury/silver alloy) filling. In the case of

Gustavus whether this dental work was carried out in his native Bavaria, in London where he worked for a period, or in New Zealand is not known. The use of gold for fillings predated the use of amalgam, which was not developed until the early 19th century (Roberts and Cox 2003), but gold continued to be used as a more expensive option. In post-medieval England, dental care was available mostly to the middle and upper classes (Roberts and Cox 2003), and the higher status of this couple in the community would be reflected in this evidence of dental care regardless of their positive identification.

Stable isotope analysis of bone collagen from the SJM burials suggests that their diet was broadly similar between individuals, based on the consumption of terrestrial crops (e.g. wheat, barley, staple vegetables), with variable amounts of domestic animal meat (pork, beef, mutton) – similar to the diet of contemporary Britain. There is some suggestion from both isotopic analysis and historical sources (*Otago Witness* 1868, 1869) that the availability of farmed meat was limited in the earliest days of the settlement. However, the availability of wild wetland resources nearby means that colonists seem to have supplemented their farmed diet to ameliorate nutritional stress in the colony (King et al 2021).

6.4. Traumatic Injuries

Injury and accidental death were common in this early colonial context, Radiography and macroscopic examination were used to identify antemortem and perimortem skeletal trauma in complete bones and fragments. Antemortem skeletal injuries occurring during an individual's life showed active or completed bone remodelling (i.e. healing). Perimortem injuries, occurring around the time of death, can be distinguished from postmortem damage by examining certain characteristics such as viscoelastic properties of fresh bone, fracture angle, lesion margins and colouration (Lovell 1997; Wheatley 2008). Traumatic lesions such as blunt force trauma (BFT) (fractures and contusions), sharp force trauma (SFT) (punctures and incisions) and dislocation of joints, were identified using the criteria defined by Byers (2002), Lewis (2008) and Šlaus et al (2012).

Traumatic injuries were observed in three of the seven (42.8%) well-preserved adults (Burials 11, 13 and 29). While the sample is small, this is a very high frequency of trauma. Most of these bone fractures occurred well before death (as shown by evidence of healing), although both historical and bioarchaeological evidence indicates that Burial 11 was killed in an accident.

Burial 11 (an adult male) had multiple antemortem and perimortem injuries. A healed fracture of his left humerus was most likely from a childhood injury (Wadsworth 1964). These types of fractures are the result of extreme varus (inward) indirect force applied to the elbow from a fall (Wadsworth 1964; Hamza et al 2019). A common complication of this injury is an outward deformity of the elbow which affects the carrying angle, restricts extension of the elbow, and can lead to numbness of the medial side of the forearm and hand (Skak et al 2001). The form of this fracture suggests abnormal development of the growth centre during healing and the bone being shorter on this side indicating the injury occurred before adolescence. However, the deformity is not severe and suggests an effective treatment of this common fracture during his childhood in England. The clinical implications of this injury suggest that B11 was partially disabled in this arm. He likely had limited straightening ability in this elbow and may have had difficulty carrying heavy weights with this arm. He may have also experienced some loss of sensation in this hand making precision movements of the hand difficult. The flattening of the tip of the left thumb may be work-related (Brickley and Buteux 2006) and risk of injury to this hand may have been increased due to the deformity of the elbow and any loss of sensation.

The perimortem injury to the right temporal region of B11's head is a linear longitudinal basal skull fracture. These fractures are invariably caused by a blow to the front or side of the head and are usually fatal if untreated as they are associated with brain-stem damage (Kerman et al 2002; Ta'ala et al 2006; Wedel and Galloway 2014). A perimortem fracture to the left thigh bone was comminuted (the shaft is broken into more than two fragments) , which is usually associated with a direct force to the bone, such as crushing (Lovell 1997; Wedel and Galloway 2014). It takes extreme force to fracture this bone and breaks are usually associated with severe blood loss from damage to associated vasculature (Clarke et al, 1955). Today, fractures of the femoral shaft are commonly associated with motor vehicle accidents, car-pedestrian collisions and plane crashes (Salminen et al, 2000; Wedel and Galloway 2014).

Due to the perimortem injuries suffered by Burial 11, alongside his age and sex, it is suspected that this is Joseph Higgins, a gold miner who died at the small mining settlement of Canada Reef in a mining accident in 1877. He was 37 years old when he died and was born in Oxford, England in c1840 (Findlay 2016). Strontium isotope analysis conducted on this individual is consistent with an origin in southern England (King et al 2020). A newspaper account of the inquest into his death describes the accident (*Bruce Herald* 13 November 1877): *One to two tons of rock and earth fell on him while he was working underground in the mine.* A schoolmaster who first attended the injured miner stated: *I noticed a wound on his temple three quarters of an inch from the left eye. Above his left ear the skull seemed to be fractured.* Despite the fact the injury to the deceased is described on the left rather than right hand side, the location of the wound is the same, and the observed fracture is consistent with this type of trauma (Kranioti 2015). No mention was made of other injuries to his body at the inquest, perhaps not surprising given the wound to his head was fatal. Joseph Higgins is also the only individual found in the historical records for

the cemetery where death occurred from such extreme trauma, further supporting his identification.

Rib fractures are most commonly associated with blunt force trauma to the chest and in modern times are often caused by motor vehicle accidents (Wedel and Galloway 2014). A 19th century equivalent could be injury associated with the use of horses (Brickley and Buteux 2006). There are numerous newspaper accounts in this period of people being killed or injured in accidents involving horses, stock and carts. Other causes of trauma to the chest are work related, assault, and interpersonal violence, especially domestic violence (Wedel and Galloway 2014). The clinical implications of rib fractures are usually overlooked in bioarchaeology as mundane, however, they signify an inability to work for some weeks at the very least, and in more extreme circumstances, life-threatening injury to organs or vessels (Brickley 2006).

Burial 11 had two rib injuries in addition to the other injuries discussed above. These occurred in separate incidents, one close to the time of death and the other was well-healed. The transverse alignment of antemortem fractures all indicate direct force causing the injury (Lovell 2000). A perimortem sharp force injury to a lower right rib fragment may have contributed to his death by damaging internal organs, and adds to the perimortem femoral and cranial fractures as evidence for his death by crushing in a rock fall.

Burial 13 (an adult male) had three well healed antemortem fractures to the ribs. These injuries represent at least one period of significant discomfort and disability during this man's life. Other possible antemortem injuries to Burial 13 include structural changes to the right femur and possibly the right tibia that may be due to a plastic deformation fracture during childhood (Glencross and Stuart-Macadam 2000). This type of fracture results in a permanent bending deformity of the affected bone without the typical callus formation (Lavery et al. 2007). However, fractures of any type to the proximal femur and affecting the hip joint are very rare in children (Brousil and Hunter 2013), and other causes such as some form of dysplasia should also be considered.

Burial 29 (an adult female) had a possible perimortem sharp force injury to the chest. This would be unlikely to have caused her death, but any other injuries to soft tissues are not visible in the skeletal record. This defect was visible during the excavation process and the margins of the break are uniformly coloured with the overlying cortex, suggesting that this occurred before the remains were interred. However, without further imaging of this trauma, it is not possible to firmly differentiate it from post mortem damage and therefore remains speculative. Her story is the subject of a separately published detailed osteobiography (Snoddy et al 2021).

The overall pattern of trauma in Burial 11 (four fractures) and Burial 13 (three, possibly five fractures) attests to repeated exposure to risks of injury throughout life. This story of injury recidivism through the life-course is not an uncommon one for this time period in England (Brickley and Buteux 2006), and in other Otago sites (Petchey et al. 2018b). Whether the childhood trauma was related to manual labour while still in Britain is unknown, but child labour was common amongst the poor and working class (Gowland et al. 2018a).

6.5. Non-Traumatic Pathology

Palaeopathology is the study of ancient disease using signs of pathology in skeletal and mummified material (Ortner 2003). Bone cells are only able to respond to pathology by either producing new bone (osteoblastic, OB) or by destroying bone (lytic, resorptive, erosive etc). The new bone pathological changes may reflect a response to specific infectious diseases such as treponemal disease, non-specific inflammation, including infections, trauma and metabolic diseases such as scurvy (Ortner 2003). Conditions that incite a destructive bone response include infectious diseases such as tuberculosis and also diseases affecting the joints such as gout. Some of these diseases may also elicit a mixed response of bone destruction in some areas of the skeleton, such as the resorptive facial lesions of leprosy and new bone production in response to inflammation in other areas; the new bone production in the lower leg of leprosy is an example of this. Because of the generalised bone response to disease, palaeopathologists use the types and patterns of bones lesions to construct a differential diagnosis of all possible causes of the lesions through a process of elimination of the least likely diseases, eventually arriving at the most likely cause (Lovell 2000). Diseases like tuberculosis can, in some cases, cause lesion types and patterns that allow a reasonably firm diagnosis in dry bone. However, in many cases it may not be possible to narrow down the cause of pathology to more than a broad category of diseases or conditions. For example, finding an individual with osteoblastic lesions of the lower leg without the distinctive resorptive changes in the facial bones would not allow a diagnosis of leprosy to be made, but may reflect a response to non-specific infection, trauma or metabolic disease (Ortner 2003).

All bones of the adult skeletons from St John's Cemetery were examined macroscopically for evidence for non-traumatic pathological changes. Some of the elements with lesions were further examined using radiography and computed tomography.

Interestingly, skeletal tuberculosis was present in only one of the individuals excavated from the cemetery (Burial 21), despite the known high tuberculosis burden in the community. Similarly, maxillary sinusitis, a skeletal marker of respiratory irritation (Roberts and Manchester 2005) was recorded in a single adult female (Burial 6). However, the poor skeletal preservation of the burials would partly explain the lack of skeletal evidence for respiratory disease among these people.

Erosive joint lesions were observed in three of the individuals (Burials 11, 13 and 29). A differential diagnosis

of these lesions would include gout and rheumatoid arthritis (Buckley 2007). In historical Europe gout was associated with dietary excess but is rarely recorded in British populations contemporary with SJM (Roberts and Cox 2003; Brickley and Buteux 2006).

6.6. Activity Related Bone Changes

Muscle attachment sites were not systematically recorded in this study, however, all individuals, including the females, displayed high robusticity indicating repeated strenuous use of muscles. Similarly, while few individuals had observable joint surfaces those that could be assessed were free of the bone changes associated with osteoarthritis. While the causes of osteoarthritis are multi-factorial, including advancing age (Arden and Nevitt 2006; Domett et al. 2017){Arden, 2006 #4238;March, 1868 #4286}, even Burial 10 (an old female) had no evidence of bony changes associated with this disease. The lack of osteoarthritis in these people is difficult to explain, as high frequencies of the disease are present in contemporary British samples (Brickley and Buteux 2006). This does also highlight the difficulties of using arthritis as a marker of activity due to its multifactorial aetiology. However, while entheseal development is not directly correlated to specific activities (Foster et al. 2014), the evidence of highly developed muscle attachment sites in most of the observable individuals suggests prolonged and strenuous general activity.

6.7. Death Certificate Information for Colonial Milton

An analysis of the death certificates of some people buried at St John's alongside the osteological evidence of health and disease has been published in Buckley et al. (2020). This analysis is based on 77 death certificates that were located from an archival search for 'Tokomairiro' or the 'Anglican burial ground'. The death certificates for others interred in the burial ground are either not extant or, because the location of burial was not recorded in some of the death registers, they could not be separated from those buried at the Fairfax cemetery. The information in the death certificates that were available provides the cause of death of 77 of the people buried at the cemetery, as well other contextual information such as place of birth, how long the person lived in New Zealand and their occupation, although this recording was by no means consistent. The TP60 group had also gathered information on other individuals buried at St John's, in some case adding to the death certificate information. A summary of the information within from both sources is provided in Table 6.3 (for infants and children) and Table 6.4 and Table 6.5 (for adults), and the analysis of causes of death (historical epidemiology) is presented in Buckley et al. (2020) and summarised briefly below.

6.8. Infant Mortality and Child-birth

Infants and children up to the age of 5 years accounted for 26% of the deceased at SJM (Buckley et al. 2020), an

Table 6.3. Summary of cause of death details for infants and children buried at St. Johns Cemetery. DC= Death Certificate. TP60=TP60 group research.

Surname	First name	Age at Death	Year of Death	Cause of Death	Source	Place of Birth	Years in NZ
Bedson	Leonard Readman	7m	1875	Pneumonia	DC, TP60	Born en route 1874	7 months
Budgen	Edward	2y 10m	1882	Drowning	DC. TP60	Milton	Entire life
Butler	Edwin	6y	1875	?	TP60	Uxbridge, Middlesex	1 year
Caudle	Stephen Jnr	1y	1865	?	TP60	Milton	Entire life
Caudle	Catherine	<1 year	1873	Whooping cough	TP60	Milton	Entire life
Caudle	Lucy	3y 4m	1873	Whooping cough	TP60	Milton	Entire life
Clegg	Frederick	15m	1877	Croup	DC, TP60	Milton	Entire life
Clegg	Frederick Thomas	3 ½ y	1887	Pthisis (TB)	DC, TP60	Milton	Entire life
Clegg	John	8m	1876	TB meningitis	DC, TP60	Glasgow	2 months
Cockerill	Annie Elizabeth	24d	1861	Natural cause	DC	Milton?	Entire life
Cockerill	Elizabeth	4y	1861	Accidental Burning	DC	Milton?	Entire life
Daniels	Alice May	9m	1876		TP60	Milton?	Entire life
Edwards	John	7y	1876		TP60	Milton?	Entire life?
Farrell	Henry Alexander	15y	1894	Pneumonia- typhoid	DC, TP60	Milton	15 years
Flahive	Mary Ann Emma	2y	1892	Accidental poisoning	DC, TP60	Milton	Entire life
Fyffe	John	19d	1879		TP60	Milton	Entire life
Mansford	Unnamed	Prem.	1857	Stillbirth?	TP60	Milton?	Entire life
Moore	Anna Bella	6y	1893		TP60	Milton	Entire life
Powley	Nanny Bradberry	27d	1862	Natural Weakness	DC, TP60	Milton	Entire life
Powley	George	15m	1877	Accidental drowning	DC, TP60	Milton	Entire life
Powley	Henry Richard	1y	1885	Pneumonia	DC, TP60	Milton	Entire life
Ronaldson	Grace Matilda	11m	1877	Endocarditis	DC, TP60	Picton	Less than one year
Snow	Levi	3y	1875	Tabes misonterica (TB)	DC, TP60	London	8 months
Taylor	Annie Phillis Franklin	2y 2m	1880	Boas Abscess (TB)	DC, TP60	Milton	Entire life
Weber	Bertha Mathilda	9m	1873		TP60	Milton	Entire life

alarming statistic in today's world but typical of the late nineteenth century. It is also possible that many of the deaths of young babies were not formally recorded.

The experiences of women expecting the birth of a child in this period was fraught with danger and uncertainty. Birth care would have been provided at home by other women in the community with limited formal training (Clarke 2012). From the 77 death certificates that have been inspected we know that at least 5 (6.4%) of women and infants died as a direct result of complications during childbirth.

The limited information that we have on the life of Flora Weber (B6) probably reflects the experiences of many early colonial women, at least in terms of the domestic duties of childbearing and childrearing are concerned (Soper 1948). Flora Weber (nee Mackay) came from a rural background in Caithness, Scotland, and arrived in Port Chalmers, New Zealand, on board the *Rajah* from London in 1853 at about the age of 15. She married Dr John Williams, who was the first medical practioner in Milton (Fulton 1922: 159), and

had six children with him, but she was widowed in 1865 at the age of 27. In 1869 Flora married Gustavus Adolphus Weber. Gustavus (known as Adolph) Weber was a native of Bavaria and had a brother living in Napier. Research suggests that he had escaped Germany with his brother, as they were pacifists (Findlay et al. 2015). They spent sometime in England as Harley street doctors and likely arrived in New Zealand in 1860 on board the *Evening Star*. Flora and Adolph probably had three children together. The first of these, Bertha Mathilda, died at 9 months of age in 1873. Another baby Linda Clementina may have survived infancy as no record is found of her related to the burial ground. The third child born to the couple was their last and tragically took the life of Flora during the birth on May 31st 1874. Flora was 36 years of age when she died of 'postpartum haemorrhage and heart disease' and the infant died the following year at 11 months of age on March 9th 1875. Flora's 17 year old daughter by her first marriage, Isabella Williams, had died the year previously of consumption. Flora's life story and the deaths of her infants are a tragic reality of the risks and heartbreak

Table 6.4. Summary of causes of death for adults buried at St. Johns Cemetery (A to O). DC= Death Certificate. TP60=TP60 group research.

Surname	First name	Age	Yr of death	Cause of death	Source	Place of birth	Years in NZ	Occupation
Albert	Olivia	35	1878	Blood loss childbirth	TP60	Ireland	19 years?	
Barrett	Jasper	73	1903		TP60	Wiltshire England	41 years	Brick kiln proprietor
Barrett	Elizabeth	52	1892		TP60			
Bennetto	Jane	51	1881		TP60	Cornwall	20 years	
Budgen	Emily	50	1893	Starvation	TP60	Sussex, Eng.	18 years	
Caudle	Stephen	68	1887		TP60	UK	26	
Clegg	Joseph	64	1877	Pleura pneumonia	DC, TP60	Bermuda 1812	14 years via Ireland til 1863	Farmer
Clegg	Mary	68	1880	Asthma	DC, TP60	County Tyrone, Ireland	17 years	
Clinton	Fanny Fynes	39	1888		TP60	Oxford, UK	15 years	
Cockerill	Mary Ann	25	1869	Abscess of Liver	DC	Milton?		
Farrell	Eleanor (Helena) Watson	40	1877	Malignant uterine tumor	DC, TP60	Belfast, Ireland	13 years	
Farrell	Peter	52	1887	Pleura pneumonia	DC, TP60	Kildare, Ireland	25 years	
Finch	Elizabeth	57	1875	Bronchitis	DC, TP60	UK	27 years	
Finch	John	83	1897	Apoplexy (stroke)	DC, TP60	Derbyshire, England	49 years	Farmer
Finch	William	25	1875	Typhoid fever	DC, TP60	Dunedin, NZ	Entire life	Bullock driver
Finch (*nee* Davy)	Mary	50	1875	Gangrene of the lung (TB)	DC, TP60	UK?	21 years	
Firman	William	51	1876		TP60	Germany USA?		
Fyfe	James	21	1899	Accidental drowning	DC, TP60	Greymouth NZ	Entire life	Farm labourer
Fyffe	John	19	1879		TP60	Milton	Entire life	
Higgins	Joseph	37	1877	Killed in a rock fall	DC, TP60	Oxfordshire, England	9 years	Gold miner
Jordan	Nita Fortescue	17	1892	Apoplexy (stroke)	DC, TP60	Wanganui, NZ	Entire life	
McDonald	Alexander Dudgeon	55	1859		TP60	Scotland	7 years	Farmer
Miller	Robert	40	1864	Hectic fever	DC, TP60	Norfolk, England	9 years	Farmer (convict in Melbourne)
Moore	Emma Sarah	71	1916	Heart failure, diabetes	DC, TP60	London	67 years	Domestic duties
Moore	John George	68	1926	Heart disease	DC, TP60	Redcastle, Scotland	47 years	Farmer
Ottrey	George	55	1898	Stomach cancer		Somerset, England	36 years	Labourer/Farmer

of motherhood in this period. Even if a child survived infancy there were ongoing environmental risks to their safety. In the St. Johns Milton records two toddlers died from accidental drowning, one from burns and another from accidental poisoning.

6.9. Adult Mortality in Milton

Generally, the historical epidemiology and osteology analyses both reflect a maturing population with a high infant mortality, which is in keeping with the historical record (Buckley et al. 2020). The relatively poor

representation of very old adults in death certificates is not surprising given the colonial context where immigrants were more likely working aged adults and their families. There are few deaths related to alcohol and accidents, which was a cause of death more common in gold mining contexts (Roberts 2006). This environment was not, however, without some specific risks. The colder months of the year brought higher death counts, and respiratory disease, particularly pulmonary tuberculosis killed over a quarter of the population. The high mortality rates from pulmonary complaints may be related to occupational health, an environmental risk

Table 6.5. Summary of cause of death details for adults buried at St. Johns Cemetery (P to W).

Surname	First name	Age	Yr of death	Cause of death	Source	Place of birth	Years in NZ	Occupation
Parker	Catherine	43	1876		TP60	Rothesay, Bute, Scot.	14 years	
Parker	Thomas		1870?		TP60			
Parker	Mary Buchanan	20	1891	Septic infection childbirth, Gout	DC, TP60	Milton	Entire life	
Parker	Mary Smyth	39	1880	Pthisis (TB) 'rupture of artery in lungs'	DC, TP60	Aberdeen, Scotland.	6 years	
Pilkington	Richard	52	1877	Mitrot regurgitation (heart valve)	DC, TP60	County Galway, Ireland	12 years	
Powley	Jane	35	1864	Consumption of the lungs	DC, TP60	Westmorland, England	11 years	
Powley	Hannorah	30	1873	Exhaustion after prem childbirth	DC, TP60	Tiperary, Ireland	10 years	Servant to John, Jane
Powley	John	67	1891	Heart disease	DC, TP60	Westmorland, England	37 years	Carter (DC) prev. farmer
Seed	John	78	1878	Atherosclerosis and stroke	DC, TP60	Born at sea	38 years	Farmer, cab. Maker,carpenter
Seed	Ann Nash	92	1893	Old age	DC, TP60	Wiltshire, England	53 years	
Shaw	Henry	37	1881	Pleuropneumonia	DC, TP60	Sheffield, England	17 years	Labourer
Shaw	Sarah Jane	19	1893	Pthisis (TB) Pulmonblis	DC, TP60	Milton	Entire life	
Shaw	Elizabeth Bell	40	1909		TP60	Milton	Entire life	
Squires	Richard Westbrooke	25	1862	TB	TP60	Liverpool, England	1 year	
Taylor	Walter	39	1881	Debilitating illness	TP60		12	Lawyer
Thompson	Robert Rowley	47	1877	Pthisis (TB) pulmondes	DC, TP60	Ireland	3 ½ years	Drill Instructor
Toogood	William	42	1873	Pneumonic pthisis haemorrhage (TB)	DC, TP60	Mitcham, Greater London	12 years via Tasmania	Gold miner, butcher, labourer, forestry
Weber	Flora Clementine	36	1874	Postpartum haemorhage	DC, TP60		21 years	
Weber	Gustavus Adolphus	44	1874	Natural causes, alcohol and chloroform	DC, TP60	Bavaria	14 years via London	Doctor
Williams	Isabella	17	1873	Consumption	TP60	Milton	Entire life	
Welham	Jane	68	1906	Apoplexy	DC, TP60	Wales, Via NSW	37 years	
Welham	George	20	1879	Coughing blood (TB)	DC, TP60	NSW	10 years	Pipe maker
Welham	William	26	1889	Pthisis (TB)	DC, TP60	NSW	19 years	Blacksmith
Woodhead	Elizabeth	66	1860	Natural decay	DC, TP60	Sheffield, England?	16 years	

factor, an epidemic or an unidentified pathogen that was not recognised at the time.

Milton was reported as having *'always a damp vapour rising, highly prejudicial to the health of the inmates, and especially the children'* (MacBean Stewart 1875). This statement may relate to the theory that disease was spread via miasma or bad air, a perception that persisted in European society until being disproven in the second half of the nineteenth century by germ theory. Pneumonia, and other respiratory complaints, were commonly listed causes of death for both sexes in the death certificates, although the higher number of cases in men may suggest an occupational health risk

(Buckley et al 2020). This picture of the environmental risks to health in the Tokomairiro plain is in stark contrast to that of Sumpter and Lewis (1949) who describe the region as too 'healthy' to offer enough sustained income for doctors seeking employment. They argue this is the reason for many doctors not staying for long periods in the town, although their stance may be a product of nostalgia given their book was one of a series of publications celebrating the centennial of the Otago Settlement.

Illnesses related to industrialisation were rife in Victorian England (Wohl 1983). Mills producing textiles were particularly dangerous, causing chronic and often fatal respiratory illness, and this has been demonstrated in the bioarchaeological record (Gowland 2018b). We know from the historical record that the township of Milton was home to various industries that were detrimental to respiratory health (flour milling, textiles, and pottery production) (Elwood 1965; Thomas and Stewart 1987; Mohammadien et al 2013). In some cases, respiratory conditions may have been contracted back 'home' in England but exacerbated by cold damp climate and unstable food resources in the early stages of the settlement. The ubiquitous evidence of tobacco use (pipe facets) in all four males and one of two females would also have contributed to respiratory disease in the population.

6.10. Summary of Bioarchaeological Evidence of Health

While the number of people excavated from the St John's burial ground was limited and mostly of very poor preservation, bioarchaeological and historical epidemiology analyses have revealed some insights into the quality of life, diet, injury and disease faced by these early settlers. Not unexpected was the picture of high numbers of infant deaths from illnesses that are largely preventable in the modern day but were ubiquitous in Victorian England and New Zealand. The detailed osteological narratives of the experiences of the adults who immigrated to New Zealand and died here reveal lives of hard beginnings and toil throughout life. This snapshot of Victorian-era life among these first generation New Zealand settlers suggests that little changed for them when they emigrated to New Zealand and they and their children remained vulnerable to old threats as well as new.

7

Material Culture

The material culture associated with the burials consisted primarily of the coffins and associated fittings (fabric covering, embossed lead/tin strip, coffin plates, handles and escutcheons, nails). It is generally the Christian tradition not to be buried with any grave goods, and nothing was found in the graves apart from some evidence of clothing (buttons, eyelets and fabric scraps), and one or two blankets with infant burials. In general the fabric coverings on the outside of the coffins were moderately-well preserved, but evidence of clothing from within the coffins was very poorly preserved. Despite this relatively sparse assemblage, the artefactual material is capable of informing us about aspects of the contemporary society, in particular the Victorian attitudes and cultural practices surrounding death and funerals.

7.1. Coffins

All of the interments were in wooden coffins, but there was considerable variation in preservation of those coffins. None survived completely intact, and in some cases the coffin dimensions were only preserved as a mould in the clay grave fill. In most cases enough of the coffin survived to allow some detailed description, but all dimensions given below (Table 7.1) are only accurate to with one or two inches because of the deterioration, and in most cases it was not possible to accurately determine the height of the coffins as they had been compressed by the grave fill. It was possible to determine that no two coffins were identical, suggesting that each was made as required to suit the person in question.

Most coffins were of the single-break form, where the widest point of the coffin is across the shoulders, and it tapers towards the head and feet, which is the traditional coffin shape still familiar today (sometimes described as 'hexagonal' as there are six, albeit unequal, sides). The exceptions to this were several smaller infant coffins that were straight-sided (one with a slight taper). Most of the coffins were covered in black fabric with pressed metal decorative strips tacked around the edge of (and sometimes across) the lids and along the sides. Iron coffin handles were present on many coffins, and these varied in the degree of ornamentation, from simple plain handles to a set of ornate cast iron handles embossed with a cherub's face. Many of the adult burials had pressed iron coffin plates on the coffin tops, and four of these still bore legible writing, allowing the confident identification of the individuals.

The discussion below considers each main aspect of coffin construction and decoration in turn. Table 7.1 summarises the main points. Dimensions are given in inches, as the coffins and coffin furniture were manufactured using imperial measurements.

7.2. Coffin Construction

All of the coffins were timber, but only ten yielded samples in good enough condition for identification. Most of these were kauri or rimu (although rimu and totara are difficult to differentiate when degraded), with one exotic conifer (probably a pine) present (Table 10). All timber identifications were carried out by Dr. Rod Wallace of Auckland.

All of the coffins were of similar construction, made from timber boards nailed together with simple butted joints. Coffin lids were simple planks cut to shape, and nailed or screwed down. Most of the timbers were rough-sawn, with circular saw marks from the sawmill still visible (Figure 7.1), varying from ½ inch (12mm) thick (for some infants) up to a maximum of 1 inch (25mm) thick for the adult in Burial 10. This burial had a notable large and heavily constructed coffin made from dressed rimu, and is discussed further below. Kerf cuts were visible in several coffins where the side boards had been partially cut through to allow them to be bent at the shoulders to create the single-break shape.

In all cases the coffins were made with the side boards overlapping the base boards, and the two were nailed together with horizontal nails, in order to ensure that the base would be strong enough to carry the weight of a body. Typically 2 inch (50mm) nails would be used for the base, and slightly shorter nails used for other joints, but there was much variation in length, and infant/child coffins tended to use shorter nails. Most of the nails recovered were iron cut nails (i.e. cut from flat iron sheet), typical of the late nineteenth century period of most of the known-age burials (Figure 7.2, Figure 7.3). A few screws were also found (Burials 11, 18, 20a, 21, 23), probably used to fix coffin lids down (Figure 7.4).

A number of the coffins also had a slight splay of the sides outwards from the base; although the preservation was in all cases too poor to observe this in the ground, analysis of nails and timber fragments from the bases of some coffins confirm this design feature (Figure 7.5). This would have added to the complexity of coffin construction, as such angled joints are more demanding to accurately make than straight right-angle butt joints.

Most of the child and baby coffins were simply a miniature version of the adult form, while two were straight-sided (either parallel sided or with a slight taper), and two were too deteriorated to determine the shape.

Table 7.1. Summary of coffin construction, decoration and dimensions. Note in the Form column 'SB' indicates a single-break shape, 'P' indicates parallel sides, and 'T' indicates a taper. All dimensions are only correct to 1 or 2 inches, due to poor coffin preservation. Coffin timber identifications by Rod Wallace.

Burial No.	Timber	Form	Covering	Metal ribbon	Coffin Plates	Length	Width (shoulders)
1	Kauri	SB	Black fabric	Y	Head, abdomen, feet	4ft 11in	14in
2		SB	Black fabric	Y	N	2ft 1in	10in
3a		SB	Black fabric	Y	N	2ft 2in	10in
3b	Rimu or Totara	SB	Black fabric	Y	N	2ft 4in	12in
4	Kauri	SB	Black fabric	Y	Head, chest, feet	6ft	20.5in
5	Prob. Rimu	SB	Black fabric	Y	Head, chest, feet	5ft 8in	20in
6	Kauri	SB	Black fabric	Y	Head, chest	6ft	19.5in
7	Kauri	SB	Black fabric	Y	Over whole lid	6ft 4in	21in
8		SB	Black fabric		N	3ft 2in	11in
9		SB	Black fabric	Y	Head, chest, feet	6ft 6in	
10	Rimu	SB	Black fabric	Y	N	6ft	26in
11		SB	Black fabric	Y	Chest	6ft 4in	20.5in
12	Not excavated						
13	Prob. Rimu	SB	Black fabric	N	Chest	6ft 2in	22in
14		P?	None	N	N	Approx 20in	?
15		?	None	N	N	Approx 20in	
16		SB	Black fabric	Y	N	3ft	11in
17		P	None	N	N	17in	11in
18	Prob. Rimu	SB	Black fabric	Y	N	2ft 9in	11in
19		SB	Black fabric	?	N	3ft	9.25in
20a		SB	Black fabric	N	N	2ft 8in	10in
20b	Exotic conifer (Pinus sp)	SB	Black fabric	N	N	3ft 6in	13in
21		SB	Black fabric	Y	Chest	6ft 5in	
22		SB	Black fabric	N	Frags?	5ft 9in	20in
23		SB	Black fabric	Y	N	6ft 4in	23in
24	Not excavated						
25	Not excavated						
26	Not excavated						
27		SB	Black fabric	Y	N	2ft 8in	10in
28		T	Black fabric	Y	Star over body	2ft 3in	10in
29		SB	Black fabric	Y	Y (frags)	6ft 3in	21in

Fig. 7.1. Rough sawn kauri in the lid of the Burial 6 coffin (Flora Weber). The pencil line visible across the board marked out the shoulder break.

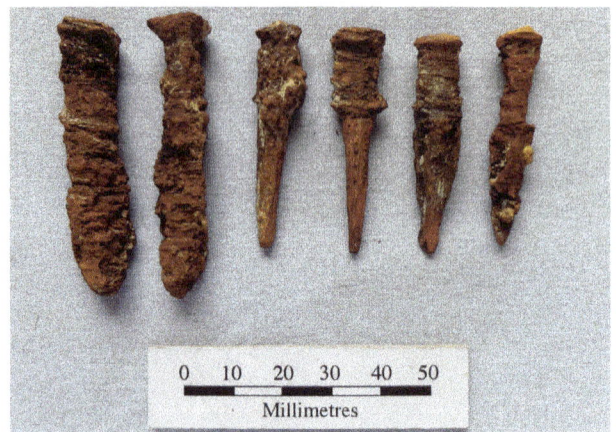

Fig. 7.2. Coffin nails from Burial 17. On left 2 ¼ inch wrought iron nails, on right 1 ¾ inch nails.

Fig. 7.3. Coffin nails from Burial 23. All are cut wrought iron nails, varying in length from 1 to 2 inches.

Fig. 7.4. Screw from the coffin of Burial 18.

Fig. 7.5. Detail of fragment from Burial 3b coffin, showing the nails that attached the coffin sides (right) to the coffin base (left). It can be seen that the coffin sides were not vertical, but were splayed out from the base.

7.3. Coffin Fabric Covering

Most coffins (all except for three infant coffins) were covered with black fabric. This was generally moderately well preserved, but with extremes of preservation, from very poor to very good (see Figure 7.6 for the best preserved example). The fabric was wrapped around the coffins and lids separately, and then fixed using small iron tacks: there was no evidence of sewn or otherwise tailored fittings. This simple way of covering and fixing was best seen in the very well preserved lid of the Burial 3a coffin, that of an infant (Figure 7.7). In many cases a decorative metal ribbon trim was then tacked on over the cloth (see next section below). One coffin (Burial 21) had evidence of painted decoration on the coffin lid (Figure 7.8), but it was too damaged and degraded to determine the design, although it was a white or light colour, and was originally quite ornate. It is possible that it was related to the role of the Ancient Order of Foresters that paid for the funeral of this individual.

Fabric samples from 21 coffins (including two samples from Burial 2, one from the lid and one from the coffin side) were analysed by Jane Batcheller of the University of Alberta (Table 11 and Appendix A). All of the samples

Fig. 7.6. The coffin lid from Burial 3a. This infant's lid was the best-preserved coffin lid found in 2016.

Fig. 7.7. The underside of the Burial 3a coffin lid, showing how the fabric was simply wrapped around the wooden lid and tacked on.

now completely degraded. The factors affecting fabric preservation in archaeological contexts are discussed in more detail below (under 'clothing') but in general protein fibres (wool and silk) tend to survive better than cellulose fibres (cotton and linen), which explains this differential preservation within a single fabric sample.

There was considerable variation in the fabrics, with plain weave, 2/1 twill, 2/2 twill, fulled and unfulled, and the already mentioned wool and wool/cotton mix all present. In most cases only a single well-reserved sample from each coffin was analysed, but both the coffin side and lid of Burial 2 were sampled and were found to be different: the lid had a heavily fulled plain weave and the side a 2/2 twill, indicating that when the coffin was made the fabric was taken from two different rolls. Conversely, the fabric on the two coffins of Burials 3a and 3b (two infants) appears to be the same, suggesting that the coffins were constructed at the same time with cloth from the same roll.

There was also some variation in the colour of the fabrics, as although most appeared black, there was at least one dark green cloth (Burial 27), one brown (Burial 28) and five with multi-coloured (although all dark) fibres (Burials 2, 4, 5, 6 and 21). However, it is unknown how dyes may have been affected by long-term burial, and it is likely that all the fabrics appeared black or nearly black when new.

Overall it appears that the actual choice of material was irrelevant so long as it appeared much the same: a black (or very dark) low-sheen fabric. The variety of fabrics represented suggests that that the local undertaker(s) did not hold a large stock of black cloth to dress the coffins, but rather purchased cloth as necessary, taking whatever was available so long as its appearance was correct. The different fabrics used for Burial 2 may suggest that the ends of odd rolls of fabric were being used up.

Fig. 7.8. A fragment of fabric from the coffin lid of Burial 21 (William Toogood) with what was once an ornate painted design.

were wool (Figure 7.9), but four samples (Burials 1, 7, 10, 14) had wool warp yarns and cotton weft yards (Figure 7.10). In all of these cases the cotton fibres were very degraded, and in addition one set of fibres from each of Burials 2 and 22 were missing, suggesting that they may also have been a wool/cotton mix with the cotton

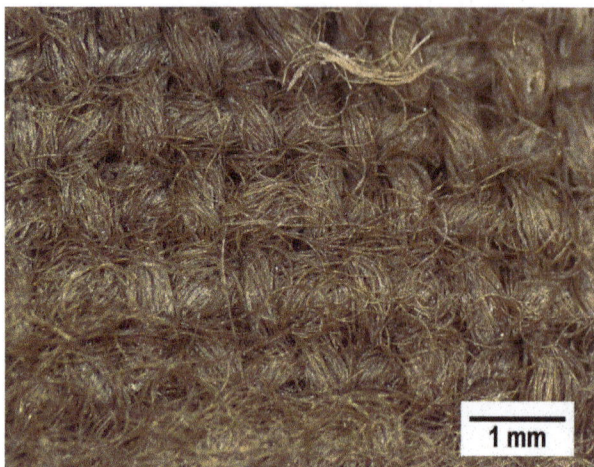

Fig. 7.9. Enlargement of the plain weave woollen coffin cloth cover from Burial 19 (Jane Batcheller).

Fig. 7.10. Enlargement of the coffin cloth from Burial 10. This is an example of a wool/ cotton mix in a 2/1 twill: the horizontal warp fibres are wool while the vertical weft fibres are cotton (Jane Batcheller).

Table 7.2. Coffin covering fabric.

Burial	Context No.	Fabric	yarn	Fibre
B1	10013	2/1 twill weave (finely woven)	wa: single, z-spun we: single, z-spun	Wa: fine wool we: cotton (degraded)
B2	10005 (lid)	Plain weave, heavily fulled.	Main yarn: single z-spun. Other yarn decomposed	Main yarn: fine and coarse wool. Dyed fibres blended (blue, green, red, natural)
B2	10005 (sides)	2/2 twill	Wa: single, z-spun We: single, z-spun	Wa: fine wool We: fine wool
B3a	10006	2/2 twill	Wa: single, z-spun We: single, z-spun	Wa: fine wool We: fine wool
B3b	10019	2/2 twill	Wa: single, z-spun We: single, z-spun	Wa: fine wool We: fine wool
B4	10018	Plain weave, heavily fulled, obscuring woven structure	Main yarn: single, z-spun	Main yarn: wool, various sizes, blue, red and natural coloured
B5	10012	Plain weave, napped or brushed on one side.	Main yarn: single, z-spun	Main yarn: wool, various sizes, blue, red and natural coloured
B6	10016	Plain weave, napped or brushed on one side.	Main yarn: single, z-spun	Main yarn: wool, various sizes, blue, red and natural coloured
B7	10014	2/1 twill weave (finely woven)	Wa: single, z-spun We: single, z-spun	Wa: fine wool We: cotton, degraded
B9	10015	2/2 twill, finely woven, traces of selvedge edge	Wa: single, z-spun We: single, z-spun	Wa: fine wool We: fine wool
B10	10028	2/1 twill	Wa: single, z-spun We: single, z-spun	Wa: fine wool We: cotton, degraded
B11	10029	2/1 twill weave	Wa: single, z-spun We: single, z-spun	Wa: fine wool We: fine wool
B13	10026	2/2 twill weave (very fine fabric)	Wa: single, z-spun We: single, z-spun	Wa: fine wool, dyed black We: fine wool, dyed black
B16	10043	2/2 twill weave	Wa: single, z-spun We: single, z-spun	Wa: wool We: wool
B18	10044	Plain weave	Wa: single, z-spun We: single, z-spun	Wa: wool, dark, dyed black? We: cotton, degraded
B19	10045	Plain weave	Wa: single, z-spun We: single, z-spun	Wa: wool, degraded We: wool, degraded
B20a	10046	2/1 twill weave	Wa: single, z-spun We: single, z-spun	Wa: fine wool We: fine wool, dyed black?
B21	10047	Plain weave, heavily fulled, brushed on one side	Main yarn: single, z-spun	Main yard: wool, various sizes, some dark coloured, red, black, blue
B22	10048	Plain weave, only one set of yarns remains	Yarns: single, z-spun	Main yarn: wool, various sizes, poor condition.
B27	10053	2/2 twill weave, green fabric	Wa: single, z-spun We: single, z-spun	Wa: fine wool We: fine wool, all fibres dyed blue
B28	10056	2/2 twill weave, tan brown	Wa: single, z-spun We: single, z-spun	Wa: fine wool We: fine wool
B29	10057	2/2 twill weave	Wa: single, z-spun We: single, z-spun	Wa: wool, various sizes, dyed black? We: wool, various sizes, dyed black?

Within the coffins no evidence of any shrouds or lining was found, although the very poor preservation of clothing (discussed below in detail) indicates that the preservation environment inside the coffins was worse than outside. Taphonomic processes that might explain this include the rapid encasing of the outer cloth in clay grave fill (reducing the oxygen available for decay) and the presence of the decaying corpse on the inside of the coffin. It is therefore not possible to say whether any coffins had internal shrouds or lining.

The fabric covering over the exterior of coffins was therefore a consistent funerary practice at SJM in the period under consideration (primarily the 1870s), with black (or very dark) wool and wool/cotton mix fabrics being used. Newspaper accounts of the time confirm that coffins usually had a black cloth covering (*Bruce Herald* 15 June 1875). These fabrics were probably purchased as required by the undertaker from a local business (presumably a tailor or haberdashery), with the main consideration being the colour, with no other standardisation. As with the other items of coffin furniture (described below), longevity was not a requirement as the coffin would soon be buried, so both heavy and light fabrics were used. There is little apparent correlation between the cloth weight and the presence/absence of other coffin furniture (such as decorative metal ribbon, coffin plates and iron handles) that might indicate social status and/or wealth. Of the three burials with ornate cast iron (and therefore presumably expensive) handles (Burials 7, 10, 29), Burials 7 and 10 both had a finely woven wool/cotton twill cover, but Burial 29 had a coarser woollen twill.

7.4. Coffin Trim Strips

Twenty three of the coffins were trimmed with embossed metal strips placed over the cloth coffin covering (Figure 7.11 to Figure 7.17). These strips (sometimes referred to as coffin lace, Mahoney-Swales et al 2011: 219) were attached using small iron tacks around the edges (and sometimes across) the lids and sides of the coffins. In all cases the trim strip was very fragile, as no metal content remained and the surviving material was simply corrosion products. As such, the best time to observe and record

these strips was in the ground before they were moved and inevitably began to disintegrate.

Analysis of the corroded remains and some matching unused strips that were located during the research (see discussion below) indicate that these were made from a lead/tin alloy, and most were unpainted, meaning that they would have had a bright shiny silver finish to contrast against the black fabric coffin coverings. One example was painted black (Burial 10, see Figure 7.17), and that coffin would have been more sombre in effect than most others. There were a wide variety of embossed designs on the strips, and they came in several widths, from ½ inch (12mm) to 3 inches (76mm), with generally the narrower strips used on the smaller infant and child coffins. All of the designs used repeating elements, often in a double row; motifs included circles, ovals, stars and cross-hatching.

During this research a set of coffin trim strips (Figure 7.18) was obtained from Trademe (the main online person to person trading platform in New Zealand), from an individual in Invercargill who was clearing out their grandparents garage and came across some antique coffin furniture, including several coffin plates (discussed below) and the strips. Although not provenanced, the strips were an exact pattern match for the strips on Burial G1 (Figure 7.19) from cemetery excavations in Lawrence (Petchey et al 2018), which was decorated in the same style as the

Fig. 7.11. Burial 1 trim. This was 1 1/8 inch (28.5mm) wide, and had a pattern of a double row of raised circles.

Fig. 7.12. The trim on the corner of Burial 2 coffin, showing how the thin metallic strip was folded to turn the corner. The corroded heads of the iron tacks used to fix the strip are also visible. The strip was 7/8 inch (22.5mm) wide, with a pattern of a double row of diamond shapes.

Fig. 7.13. Burial B3a trim. This trim strip was 7/8 inch (22.5mm) wide.

Fig. 7.14. Burial 4 coffin trim. This trim was 1 ½ inches (38mm) wide, with a double row of a cursive (foliage?) pattern. It was poorly preserved.

Fig. 7.15. Embossed metal trim on the lid of Burial 6 (Flora Weber). This strip was 1 ½ inches (38mm) wide, with a double row of raised ovals pattern.

Fig. 7.16. Embossed metal trim on the Burial 9 (Robert Rowley Thomson) coffin. This strip was 1 ½ inches (38mm) wide, and appears to be identical to Burial 6 (Flora Weber).

Fig. 7.17. The black enamelled embossed metal ribbon used to embellish the coffin of Burial 10. This strip was 3 inches (76mm) wide, with a double row of stars and cursive surrounds. This was the only black-coloured trim strip found at SJM.

Fig. 7.18. Embossed metal trip strip obtained from Trademe in 2019. This is an exact match for an archaeological example from Lawrence Burial G1 (following Figure). This strip is a maximum of 2 inches (50mm) wide and was supplied in 12 inch (305mm) lengths.

Fig. 7.19. The coffin strip on Burial G1 from the Gabriel Street Cemetery in Lawrence. This is exactly the same pattern as in Figure 7.18 above, and illustrates the difference between the original appearance and the degraded appearance of the archaeological samples.

Milton coffins. This allowed the material to be identified (a lead-tin alloy, similar to pewter or electrical solder), and the original appearance to be appreciated (Figure 7.18). While not an exact match for any of the Milton trim, the style is consistent with the decorated Milton coffins.

The 23 trimmed coffins out of 27 individual burials represents 85% of the sample. Adult burials were most likely to have trimmed coffins (8 with, 3 without), but slightly more than half of the infants and children also had trimmed coffins (9 with, 7 without), indicating that this was a consistent funerary treatment that was applied to both adults and children.

7.5. Coffin Plates

Coffin plates (also known as depositum plates) were thin pressed metal plates attached to tops of many of the coffins. There would typically be one, two or three plates: one over the chest (the main and sometimes only one), one over the head and one over the feet. The plates served two main purposes: a decorative purpose (although some plates were also ascribed symbolic meanings) and a formal identification purpose as the deceased's name would be inscribed on the chest plate. Some public cemeteries had a formal requirement to have an identification plate on the coffin: the *1864 Cemetery Reserves Management Ordinance* (*Otago Ordinances*, Session XVIII, No. 146, 1864) required mangers of public cemeteries to make rules and regulations for those cemeteries, and at the Lawrence Cemetery (also being studied by the Otago Cemeteries Archaeology Project) one particular rule (No. 11) stated that '…every coffin in a private grave must have on the lid a lead or copper plate, with the name of the deceased stamped thereon' (*Otago Provincial Gazette,* Vol. 10 No. 407, 14 February 1866: 33-34). At Lawrence most of the burials investigated in 2018 and 2019 had no name plates, and those that did were on thin pressed iron, the same as found at St. John's Cemetery. None were on lead or copper as the rules stated. Rules for the St. John's Cemetery have not yet been found (it was a Church cemetery not a public cemetery), but it is likely that a similar requirement for a named coffin plate did exist.

Ten coffins at SJM had evidence of coffin plates, most on adult burials with just two on child burials (Table 7.3). These ranged from largely complete items upon which the name of the deceased could still be read (four individuals), to just fragments of corrosion. All of the plates were of the same material: thin pressed iron sheet (originally tin plated) with a black enamelled finish, and the name of the deceased written in gold paint on the main chest plate. The numbers of plates per coffin varied: from a single plate over the chest, to almost the entire lid covered with plates (Burial 7). The most common pattern was for there to be a main plate over the chest, with additional smaller plates over the head and/or feet. The typical mid-Victorian layout would be a main chest plate (with name and age of deceased), an angel plate over the head and a flower vase (or 'flowerpot') plate over the feet (Hoile 2018: Figure 1; Miles and Connell 2012: Figure 42), which is the arrangement on the best-preserved coffin plates at SJM, that of Burial 9 (Robert Rowley Thompson).

Thompson's main chest plate (Figure 7.20) was a large ornate pressed iron plate, black enamelled and with gold lettering painted on a central shield ('Robt. R Thompson, Aged 47 Years'). On either side of the shield was an angel, and above the shield was a crown bearing the embossed legend 'GLORIA DEO' (Glory to God), and above the crown several cherubs (in other words, the plate was heavily laden with Christian imagery). This main coffin plate was almost identical in design to the type CAS 38 recorded in five examples in the New Bunhill Fields burial ground in London (Miles and Connell 2012: Figure 28 and Table 12). The illustrated example from this site was for Mrs. Susannah Haskell, who died in 1833 at the age of 50. Like Thompson's plate at St. John's Susannah Haskell's plate was finished in black, but hers was engraved with her details while Thompson's was painted in gold lettering. Thompson also had an angel plate over the head (Figure 7.21), and the remains of a vase and flowers over the feet.

Augustus Weber's (Burial 4) and his wife Flora Weber's (Burial 6) coffin plates were equally ornate (Figure 7.22, Figure 7.23), although more corroded so that details of the designs were not so visible. Both had the standard central shield for the name and age, and it is likely that both were flanked by angels. Dr Weber (B4) also had an angel head plate and possibly a vase-shaped foot plate as well, while Flora Weber (B6) appears to have had the main chest plate and a head plate (very fragmented).

The plate on Burial 5 (unidentified) was more restrained, with the shield present but with far less surrounding ornamentation (Figure 7.24). This may have been the

Table 7.3. Coffin plates found at St. John's Cemetery in 2016. Plates marked as 'fragments' were too deteriorated to describe.

Burial No	Context No	Head	Chest	Feet
1 (child)	10013	Fragments	Fragments	Fragments
4 (Gustav Weber)	10018	Angel	Ornate shield	Flower vase?
5 (older child)	10012	Fragments	Shield	Fragments
6 (Flora Weber)	10016	Fragments	Ornate shield	
7 (adult)	10014	Fragments	Large ornate urn-shaped plate with figure	Fragments
9 (Robt Thompson)	10015	Angel	Ornate shield	Flower vase
11 (adult)	10029		Shield (poor)	
13 (adult)	10026		Shield (large, poor)	
21 (William Toogood)	10047		Shield (poor)	
29 (adult)	10057		Large Shield? (poor)	

Fig. 7.20. The Burial 9 coffin plate after careful cleaning. The name 'Robt. R. Thompson' is legible.

Fig. 7.22. Burial 4 coffin plate (Augustus Weber).

Fig. 7.21. The angel headplate on Robert Rowley Thompson's coffin (Burial 9).

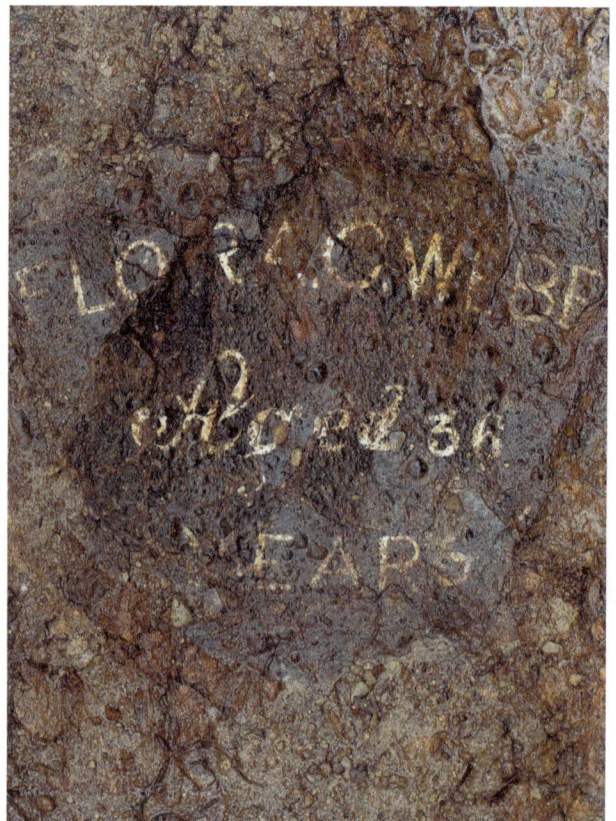

Fig. 7.23. Detail showing the text on the Burial 6 Coffin Plate for Flora Weber.

Fig. 7.24. The Burial 5 coffin plate. Traces of gold paint could be seen, but the name of the deceased could not be determined. This is an example of a simpler shield form, with garlands around the sides rather than flanking angels as seen in larger plates.

Fig. 7.25. The main coffin plates on Burial 7. The best-preserved was the main chest plate, shown in more detail in the following Figure.

grave of a child, and was the smallest coffin to have a coffin plate.

The largest and most ornate example of coffin plate decoration was on Burial 7 (which also had ornate cast iron handles, see discussion below). On this coffin lid the ornamental plates stretched in an unbroken line from just below the head down to over the feet (Figure 7.25, Figure 7.26). No name was legible, and the preservation of the plates was poor, but the main chest plate probably had a large central figure dressed in robes. One taphonomic consequence of the B7 plates in particular was that any part of the skeleton underneath an iron plate was very degraded.

Burial 13 also had a large coffin plate, but all internal detail was lost to corrosion (Figure 7.27).

The imagery in the Milton coffin plates all reflects Christian ideas of Resurrection, including angels, crowns, cherubs, and radiance. Numerous matches in general design have been made between coffin plates found in the St. Johns Cemetery and examples found in British excavations (e.g. see Miles and Connell 2012: Fig. 38). In general the funerary material culture appears to reflect nineteenth century British tradition, both in Britain and

in other British colonies (Cowie et al 2008; Hoile 2018; Mahoney-Swales et al 2011: 221; Miles and Connell 2012; Pearson et al 2011).

The various items of coffin furniture, including the plates, coffin handles (discussed in the following section) and embossed trim (discussed in the preceding section) were all mass-produced, with Birmingham being a particular centre of manufacture (Holie 2018). Funeral directors could order this material from trade catalogues, and Hoile (2018) considers that these directors were more influential in determining coffin furniture fashion than individual customers (i.e. relatives of the deceased). Many of the coffin plate designs were used with little change over a very long period of time, in some cases from the late eighteenth until the early nineteenth centuries (Hoile 2018: 218). In the case of St. John's Cemetery the similarity of the coffin plate of Robert Rowley Thompson, who died in 1877 with the coffin plate of Mrs. Susannah Haskell who died in 1833 in London (Miles and Connell 2012: Figure 38) illustrates this: a 44 year gap between the two burials had no effect on the coffin plate imagery.

Fig. 7.26. Detail view of the main chest plate on the Burial 7 coffin. A figure with radiance above stands atop the urn-shaped area where the deceased's name would have been painted.

Fig. 7.27. Burial 13 showing the large coffin plate over the chest. The outline of the plate could be determined, but most internal detail was lost in the mass of corrosion.

7.6. Coffin Handles

Coffin handles (also referred to as 'grips') were found on 11 coffins, eight adults and three infants/children (Table 7.4). They were all made from cast iron, and can be divided into two broad classes: plain iron handles with no decoration; and ornate iron handles. All were of the swing-bail form, whereby they were pivoted where they were joined to the coffin so that they could be swung out by the pallbearers to carry the coffin. The other main types of handles are short bar handles, where a bar is solidly mounted on lugs leaving sufficient space for pallbearers' hands, and rope handles where loops of rope were passed beneath the coffin. No bar handles were found at SJM, and no evidence of rope handles survived (one example of rope handles was found at the Ardrossan St Cemetery in Lawrence in 2018, report in preparation).

A selection of handles was cleaned in the laboratory to allow the decorations to be recorded, and a sample was also X-rayed. The X-ray images not only allowed the handle outlines to be seen through corrosion conglomerations, but also gave an idea of the quality of the iron used, as areas where no metallic iron remained could be determined from those where metal survived.

Table 7.4. Coffin handle summary.

Burial No	Name/Age	Handle material and description	Number of handles on coffin
1	Child	Plain cast iron, 4.5 inches wide	6
4	Gustav Weber	Plain cast iron, 5 inches wide.	6
7	Adult male	Ornate cast iron, 5.5 inches wide.	
8	Child	Plain cast iron, 3 inches wide.	4
9	Robert Rowley Thompson (47 years)	Plain cast iron, 5 inches wide.	6
10	Adult (female)	Ornate cast iron (cherub face), 6.75 inches wide.	7
11	Adult (male)	Plain cast iron, 5 inches wide.	4
21	William Toogood	Plain cast iron, 4.5 inches wide.	6
23	Adult (female)	Plain cast iron.	8
27	15 months	Small plain cast iron, 2.5 inches wide.	4
29	Adult (female)	Ornate cast iron (V shape), 6.75 inches wide.	8

7.6.1. Plain Handles

Eight sets of plain cast iron handles were found (see Figure 7.28 to Figure 7.32 for a sample). All were of a very similar shape, but they ranged in size from 2.5 inches (63mm) wide on an infant coffin (Burial 27) to 5 inches (127mm) wide on several adults. Children/infants only had plain handles, while adults had both plain and ornate (see below) handles. The state of preservation varied, and it was found that the more gracile plain handles broke easily. For this reason the handles were mainly X-rayed rather than mechanically cleaned. Figure 7.29 shows an X-ray of a well-preserved handle, while Figure 7.31 shows handles with little metallic iron remaining.

7.6.2. Ornate Handles

Three sets of ornate cast iron handles were found, all on adult burials (Burials 7, 10, 29). These contrasted greatly to the plain handles discussed above: not only were they considerably more ornate, but they were also much larger and heavier than the plain handles. All three burials had different designs, (Figure 7.33 to Figure 7.38). Pressed iron escutcheon plates (or grip plates) were mounted on the coffin sides to back the handles, and although most of these were badly degraded it was possible to determine that they had been ornate in a similar style to the coffin plates.

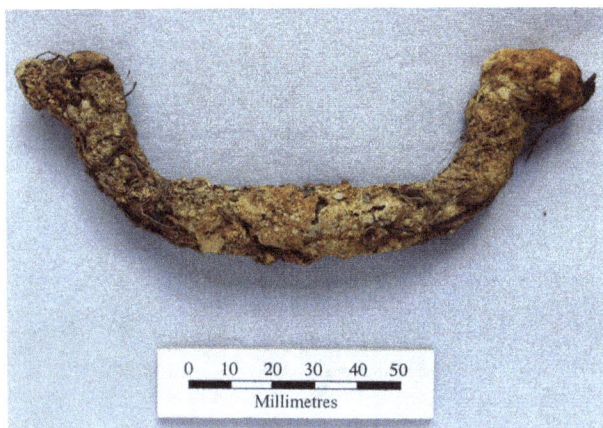

Fig. 7.28. Burial 4 coffin handle, uncleaned. This was one of the handles on Gustav Weber's coffin, and is typical of the plain cast iron handles found at St. Johns Cemetery.

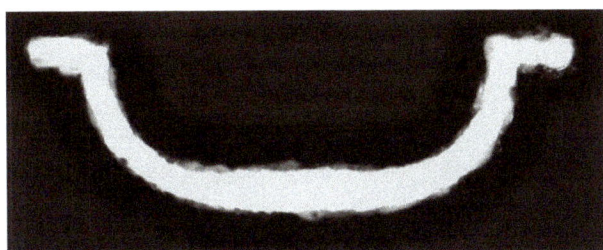

Fig. 7.29. Burial 4 coffin handle x-ray, showing the original form of the handle without cleaning being required (Pacific Radiology).

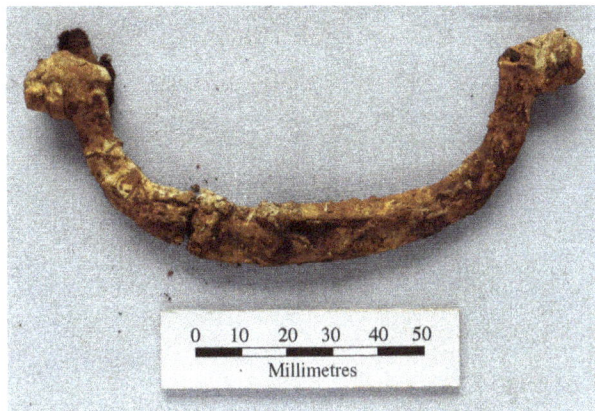

Fig. 7.30. Burial 21 coffin handle. Handle from William Toogood's coffin.

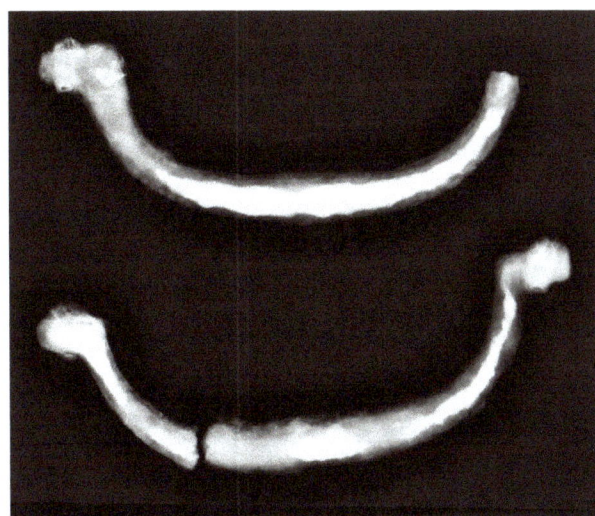

Fig. 7.31. X-ray of Burial 21 coffin handles, showing how the iron had corroded until there was only a thin core of metal (Pacific Radiology).

Fig. 7.32. Burial 23 coffin handle after mechanical cleaning in the laboratory.

Burial 7 handles had ornate bail and single central lug in a stylised cross. These handles were still in excellent condition, and when cleaned were found to be as solid and strong as when new. The Burial 10 handles had ornate bails with a central motif of a human face, but simple plain lugs.

Fig. 7.33. Coffin handle from Burial 7, with the right half cleaned to expose the decorative iron casting, and the bail and lug separated. This handle was still sound and solid, as can be seen from the intact swivel pins.

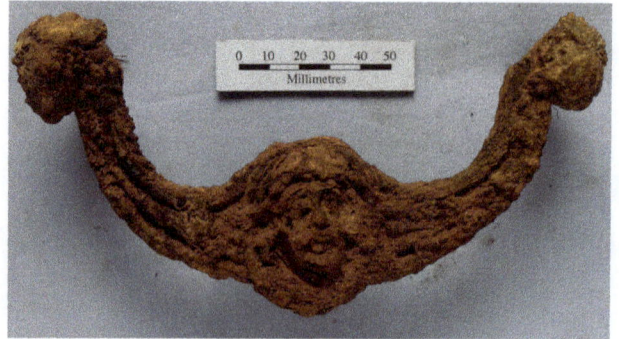

Fig. 7.35. One of the ornate cast iron handles from the coffin of Burial 10. These handles were ornate but the cast iron was heavily corroded, and details of the design were degraded. The handles had a face in the centre.

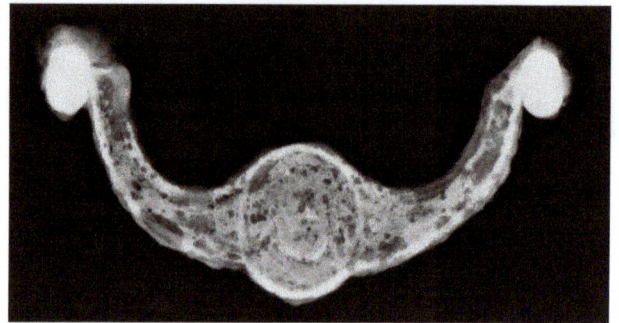

Fig. 7.36. Burial 10 coffin handle x-ray. Extensive areas of deep corrosion of the iron can be seen (darker areas) (Pacific Radiology).

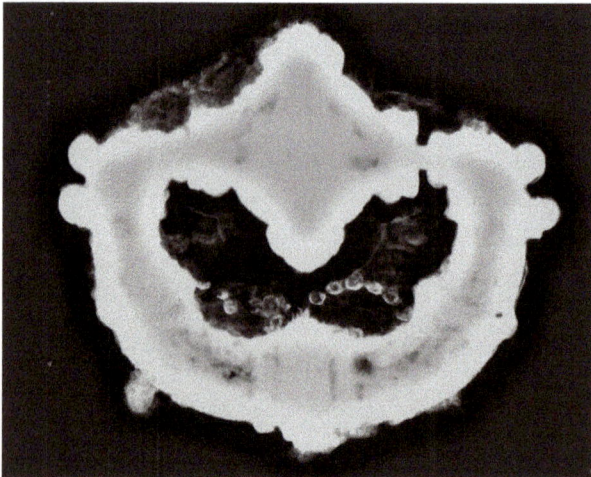

Fig. 7.34. Burial 7 coffin handle x-ray. The thinner metal through the centre of the handle can be seen (darker grey area): the handle was cast with a semi-hollow back. A section of the decoration on the escutcheon plate can also be seen (the semi-circular row of dots within the area enclosed by the handle).

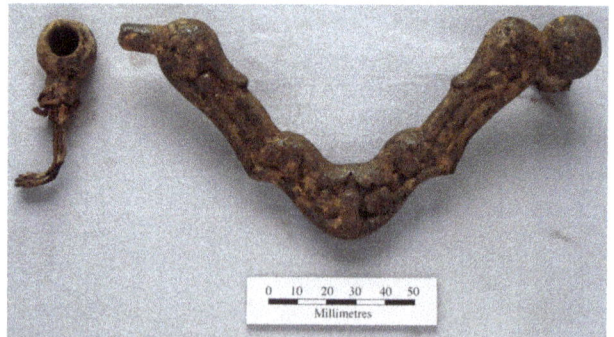

Fig. 7.37. Burial 29 coffin handle, cleaned and with one hinge open to show the hinge pin. This cast iron handle was still in sound condition.

The handles were badly corroded, and even after careful cleaning the design was degraded (the handles were too thick for X-rays to provide details of the design other than the outlines of the bails). The Burial 29 handles were the simplest of this group, with plain lugs and basic V-shaped bails with some detailing. These handles were in excellent condition.

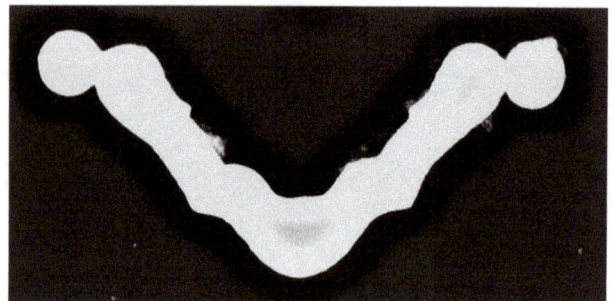

Fig. 7.38. Burial 29 coffin handle x-ray, showing that the handle is intact and the iron is in sound condition (Pacific Radiology).

7.7. Overall Coffin Design and Construction

The details of coffin construction, finish and ornamentation described above all combine to produce an overall picture of coffin construction and ornamentation as practised in Milton in the 1870s, and this can then be compared to other archaeological evidence from New Zealand and internationally. Apart from some of the smallest infant burials all of the coffins at SJM followed a distinctive style with the traditional single-break shape used for all of the adult and most of the child coffins, with a simpler rectangular or trapezoid shape used for a few of the smallest infant coffins. Almost all coffins (apart from three infants) at SJM were then covered in black (or very dark) fabric. After that there was more variation, with combinations of embossed metal trim, coffin plates and handles applied, but the overall funerary style and approach was consistent: the changes were in the size of the coffins and in the amount and intensity of the decorative elements.

Ordinary milled timber was used for most coffins at SJM, particularly the New Zealand natives rimu and kauri, these species used being common in the construction and joinery industries (in the UK elm was a traditional timber for coffin construction). The timber was in most cases rough-sawn (i.e. unfinished) as the almost ubiquitous fabric coverings meant that the timber surface was not visible.

The variation in coffin size and detail indicates that each was constructed individually, presumably made to order to suit the deceased. It is likely that old western movie trope of the undertaker measuring up the condemned man has a grain of truth in it. Where age estimation based on human remains was possible this estimate matched the overall coffin size (adults were in the largest coffins, older children in the middle-sized, and infants in the smallest). Given this consistent patterning in several instances the size of infants' coffins was used to estimate their general age in the absence of any preserved skeletal remains. Coffin size is also of note in the case of Burial 10, as the 6 ft (1.83m) length was at the lower end of the range for adult coffins but it was the widest coffin found at 26 inches (660mm) across the shoulders, and was constructed from heavy 1 inch thick timbers. The skeleton of the (female) individual was quite gracile, and not tall (estimated height 5 feet 2 inches, 158cm), but was found with her arms widely splayed at the sides. It seems likely that she was obese in life, and the coffin was made to suit, and is now the only evidence of this aspect of her physical health. Burial 23 was similar in many regards, with the second widest coffin (23 inches, 590mm), and was also probably a large and heavy individual.

The appearance of the coffins was consistent, all being wrapped in dark fabric with various degrees of ornamentation. No two were identical, but all followed a basic stylistic formula, common to both adults and children (Figure 7.39). The embossed metal (lead/tin alloy) trim (used in 23 of the 27 coffins) was used to outline the lid, and then variously also used across the lid and on the sides. Several infant and child coffins were decorated in the same way as adult coffins, the main apparent constraint being size: Burial 3b had an elaborate application of trim around and across the lid (Figure 7.39). Coffin plates and handles were present mainly on adult coffins, but three child coffins were fitted with iron handles (possibly purely ornamental as they appear to be too small to have actually been used to carry the coffin), and two older child coffins had coffin plates. The coffin plates (of thin pressed and painted tinplate) and some of the handles (cast iron) were adorned with decoration that was typical of the period and comparable to overseas (and especially British) examples, with angels, cherubs, flowers and other motifs that were intended to be symbolic of Christian salvation and resurrection.

Comparison with archaeological evidence from other cemetery excavations places the SJM funerary practice (which dates mainly to the mid-1870s) firmly within that typical of the late nineteenth century Anglo world. The single-break coffin shape is almost ubiquitous, and coffin construction using kerf cuts at the shoulder break has also been recorded in the UK when good preservation conditions have allowed, suggesting continuity in carpentry practices as well as funerary fashion (Mahoney-Swales et al 2011: 218). Eighteenth and nineteenth century burials recorded in Chelsea, Southwark (both in London), Sheffield, and even on the island of St. Helena have all revealed similar funerary practices, including fabric-covered coffins finished with trim strips and coffin plates (Cowie et al 2008; Hoile 2018; Mahoney-Swales et al 2011: 219, 221; Miles and Connell 2012; Pearson et al 2011). The thin pressed-iron coffin plates in particular are widely recorded (they are often a focus of reports because of their decorative nature and the names that can sometimes be read) and the SJM examples are also consistent with British examples, in Sheffield and London, although base-metal examples (lead or copper alloy) were also found in there but were absent at SJM (e.g. see Miles and Connell 2012).

In Australia, New Zealand's closest Anglo-world neighbour, excavations at the Old Sydney Burial Ground in 1974, 1991 and 2008 found evidence of similar coffin shape and nailed construction, also using locally-native timbers, with possible evidence that some of the coffins were also fabric-covered (preservation was poor). This was an older cemetery, in use between 1792 and 1820, and coffin decoration was simpler without the use of coffin lace and iron handles were conspicuously absent, a few coffins instead being decorated using brass tacks (Lowe and Mackay 1992: 19; Pitt et al 2017: 15-17, 19). This was a first-generation cemetery (using Deed's 2015 categorisation), and so the simpler treatment can be ascribed to both earlier styles and a simpler frontier treatment. Nevertheless, the similarities in coffin style and treatment appear consistent with eighteenth and nineteenth century British and Anglo-world funerary tradition.

In New Zealand the number of comparable archaeological samples is small. The most detailed examination of historic New Zealand funerary practice has been based on examination of above-ground features and found aspects of both imported and locally-evolved tradition (Deed 2015), but in-ground archaeological investigations are few and under-reported. The two largest cemetery exhumation projects at Symonds Street in Auckland (1967) and Bolton Street in Wellington (1969-70) were both carried out for motorway construction, and neither involved archaeological investigation or recording (Best and Furey 2006: 21). But smaller and more recent excavations have been recorded, and similar contemporary funerary traditions to SJM have been observed at several sites including the Westney Road Denominational Graveyard in Auckland, the Withells Road Cemetery in Christchurch, and recent excavations at Lawrence and Drybread in Otago.

The Westney Road Denominational Graveyard in Auckland was excavated in 2006 in order to exhume the burials to allow airport expansion. A total of 32 burials were found, although the opportunities for osteological study were very limited. In common with SJM this cemetery also catered to a small rural population with most burials in the period from 1870 to 1900, and showed similar coffin treatment in many aspects (Best and Furey 2006). There coffins were also mostly of the single-break form (referred to by Best and Furey as 'pinchfoot' because the foot end is slightly narrower than the head end), covered in fabric, trimmed with embossed metallic strips, and with cast iron handles. However, although several of the handles found there were similar in style to Burial 7 at SJM there was a larger number and wider variety of ornate handles than at SJM (see Best and Furey 2006: Figures 11 and 12), while conversely there were far fewer coffin plates found; only two were recorded from the 32 total burials. Also, several examples of decorative coffin fastenings were found at Westney Road (Best and Furey 2006: Figure 9), while none were found at SJM.

The Withells Road Cemetery was a long disused Wesleyan (Methodist) graveyard that was excavated in 1981 in order to allow the land to be sold off for development by the Church (Trotter and McCulloch 1989). Thirteen burials were excavated, with the known dates of interment being between 1871 and 1894. The funerary treatments were again consistent with the contemporary SJM burials, with fabric-covered coffins, patterned metal trim strips, metal coffin plates and cast iron coffin handles (Trotter and McCulloch 1989: 8-14). Two of the coffin plates could be read, enabling the individuals to be identified. The report is not illustrated, but several of the coffin plates were described as 'shield-shaped.'

The present Southern Cemeteries Archaeological project has recently conducted excavations in Lawrence and Drybread in Otago (Petchey et al 2018 and reports in preparation), and a range of coffin treatments have been found. A number of plain unadorned wooden coffins were found at the goldrush-era Ardrossan Street Cemetery in Lawrence and at Drybread, and this is interpreted to be the result of frontier-period burials in the former case and poor burials in the latter case. Coffins furnished in a similar fashion to the SJM examples, with black fabric covering, trim strips, coffin plates and cast iron handles, and tentatively dated to the 1870s to 1890s, were found at the Gabriel Street Cemetery in Lawrence and at Drybread, representing a more settled community and individual affluence.

There is also some historic photographic evidence for this overall style of coffin decoration, as the mass grave for the victims of the Brunner Mine Disaster of 1896 was photographed, clearly showing the tops of 26 coffins (Figure 7.40). Although taken 20 years after the SJM burials discussed here, the coffins appear to have been decorated in an identical style. The image clearly shows black (or very dark) coffins with trim along the edges of the lids and also sometimes across the lids in various patterns, and a range of coffin plates with the chest plate dominating in most cases. This minor variation of details within a number of burials on the same date demonstrates how the SJM burials with their minor variations can all be considered to be within the same overall tradition. It also demonstrates how little this tradition appears to have changed over the last three or four decades of the nineteenth century.

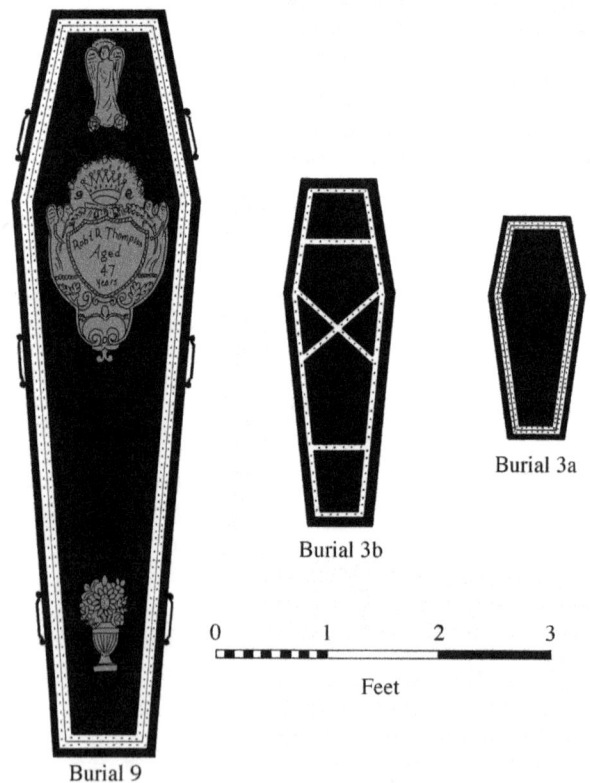

Burial 3a

Burial 3b

Burial 9

Fig. 7.39. Reconstruction of the appearances of the coffins of Burials 3a, 3b and 9 (Robert Rowley Thompson) from St John's Milton, based on archaeological evidence. Adult, child and baby coffins all followed the same basic fashion, with complexity increasing with physical size and (presumably) wealth.

Fig. 7.40. The mass grave for the Brunner Mine Disaster victims, 1896. Although this funeral occurred 20 years after most of the known SJM burials, it can be seen that the style of coffin decoration was almost identical (Christchurch City Libraries, CCL-PhotoCD02-IMG0073).

7.8. Clothing and Other Textiles

While the fabric exterior coffin coverings described above were moderately well preserved, evidence of clothing and any other fabric within the coffins was very poorly preserved. There were a few solid objects such as buttons, but otherwise only small fragments of clothing were found. There was no evidence of footwear found in any grave. As leather generally survives well in both wet and dry archaeological contexts, and well-preserved leather boots were found in some Chinese graves in Lawrence (Petchey et al 2018), it is almost certain that none of the individuals that were investigated at SJM were buried wearing shoes. Included here, although not technically clothing, Burial 15 (a baby) appears to have been wrapped in a woollen blanket within the coffin. The blanket was a plain weave with an open structure, and was in a very degraded condition.

The clothing evidence that was found was identified by Jane Batcheller and is summarised in Table 7.5 and Table 7.6. It consisted of fabric fragments from four burials (Burials 7, 9, 15, 21), and buttons from five burials (Burials 7, 13, 16, 20a, 29). Most of the fabric samples were woollen, with only a ribbon from Burial 21 being silk.

Table 7.5. Clothing Fabric.

Burial	Context No	Description	Fabric
B7	10014	Fabric tape	Narrow braid with oblique interlacing. Yarns: 2-ply, zzS-spun. Fine and coarse wool, all white.
B7	10014	Cloth, raised nap	Plain weave, heavily fulled and napped or brushed.* Main yarn: singe z-spun. Wool fibres in blue, red, natural and maybe black.
B9	10015	Cloth.	2/2 twill weave, fulled but not napped. Warp and weft single s-spun. Both fine wool.
B15	10042	Blanket? Over body	Plain weave, open structure. Warp and weft single, s-spun. Both wool.
B21	10047	Ribbon over maxilla	Fine braided, oblique interlacement. Yarns single, no twist, multi-filament silk, dyed bright blue.

* Fulled: fabric was washed and washed and beaten during manufacture to thicken the cloth.
Napped: the surface fibres of the cloth have been teased or raised.
Twill: textile weave with a pattern of diagonal parallel ribs.
Warp and weft: the longitudinal and transverse yarns in a woven fabric.

Table 7.6. Clothing fittings.

Burial	Context No	Description	Comments
B7	10014	Iron 4 hole pressed button, 0.5 in dia.	Sewn to woollen fulled and napped cloth.
B7	10014	Fragments of possible brass eyelet or button ring, found over hips.	Very fragmented.
B13	10026	3 metal buttons, fabric covered, 0.5 in dia.	
B16	10043	Brass eyelet or button ring, 5/8 in dia. Found under vertebra.	Some traces of fabric on eyelet.
B20a	10046	Possible button.	Very fragmented.
B29	10057	4 brass eyelets or button rings, 3/5 in dia. Traces of fabric.	Some traces of fabric. Probably brass rings to support fabric covered buttons.

Burial 7 had the most surviving material, consisting of a small piece of fulled woollen cloth with a raised nap and a ½ inch diameter 4 hole pressed iron button attached (Figure 7.41), together with a length of woollen tape (Figure 7.42). The cloth and button appeared to be a fragment of an exterior garment, but it is not possible to be any more precise. The use of the tape was not apparent, but it could have been used for edging or binding a garment seam. Although the archaeological sample appears brown, microscopic analysis suggested that it was originally white.

Burial 9 was the only grave with an identified individual found with clothing remains. This was Robert Rowley

Fig. 7.41. A fragment of woollen cloth that has been heavily fulled and napped, with a ½ inch pressed iron button, from Burial 7. The scale is in 0.5mm increments.

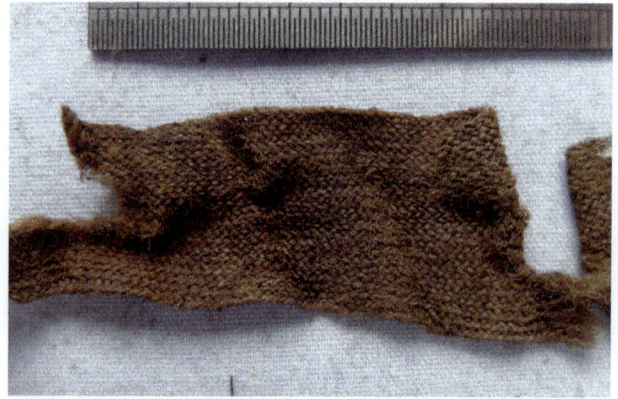

Fig. 7.42. The piece of woollen fabric tape from Burial 7. The scale is in 0.5mm increments.

Thomson, who died in 1877. He was a staff-sergeant in the No. 2 Battalion of the Otago Rifles, and was buried with full military honours (*Bruce Herald* 11 September 1877), raising the interesting possibility that he may have been buried in his uniform. His coffin was covered in a wool 2/2 twill weave cloth, but fragments of an obviously different fulled 2/2 twill weave cloth were found (Figure 7.43), one of which appeared to have a sewn seam. Examples of contemporary local volunteers uniforms held in the Otago Settlers Museum in Dunedin are also of a fulled woollen fabric and not all of these items had metal buttons (which would have left some archaeological evidence), and therefore while the archaeological evidence is far from conclusive, it does remain a possibility that Thompson was buried in uniform.

Burial 21 contained several pieces of black silk ribbon found over the maxilla. One well-preserved section was still tied in a bow (Figure 7.44, Figure 7.45). It was not clear whether this was a bow tie or a silk bow otherwise associated with funeral decoration of the body or casket.

Other clothing was only represented by hardware fittings. Burial 13 contained three ½ inch diameter fabric covered

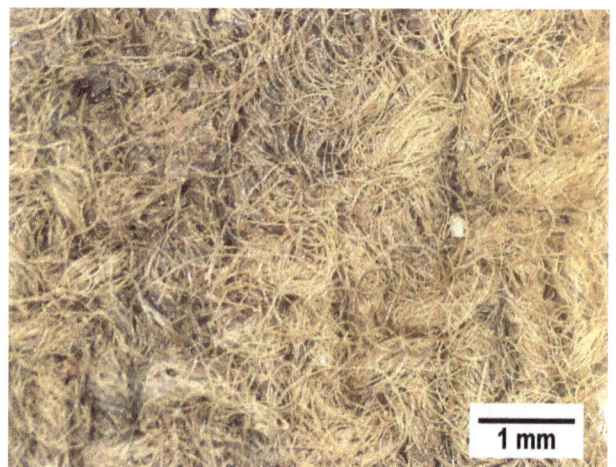

Fig. 7.43. Magnified image of fulled woollen cloth from Burial 9 (Jane Batcheller).

Fig. 7.44. Bow tied in silk ribbon from Burial 21.

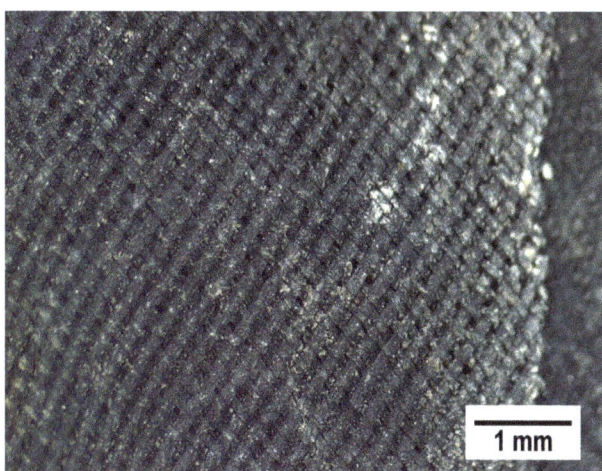

Fig. 7.45. Enlargement of the silk braid of the ribbon from Burial 21 (Jane Batcheller).

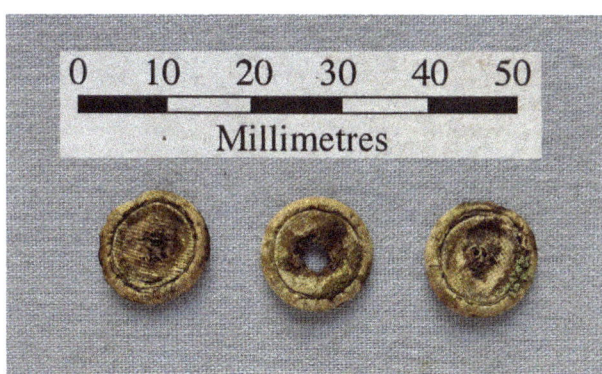

Fig. 7.46. Three ½ inch diameter fabric covered buttons found over the chest of Burial 13.

buttons (Figure 7.46). These would originally have been white, and were probably shirt buttons, as they were found over the chest area and Burial 13 was probably male. An alternative interpretation is that they were shroud buttons. Burials 16 and 29 both contained metal rings that bore traces of finely woven fabric (probably cotton) that had been preserved where it had been in contact with the metal

(Figure 7.47, Figure 7.48). These were probably the brass rings used to support the shape of fabric buttons. Once again, these could be from a garment such as a nightshirt or from a shroud.

Overall there was evidence that some of the individuals at SJM were buried in day clothes, while others were possibly buried in lighter cotton nightshirts or shrouds. In early nineteenth century Britain burial in shrouds appears to have been more common than in personal day clothes (Mahoney-Swales et al 2011: 224), meaning that this was also a possibility in New Zealand, but the evidence from SJM was too fragmentary to make any definitive statements.

There are probably several reasons for this scant evidence of clothing. If some of the individuals had been dressed in lightweight garments such as cotton nightshirts or shrouds when they were buried, these would have deteriorated rapidly. No shroud pins were found at SJM, but some of the buttons may have been from shrouds.

Fig. 7.47. A metal (probably copper alloy) ring from a fabric covered button from Burial 16. Traces of a finely woven fabric (probably cotton) have been preserved where they touched the metal. The scale increments are 0.5mm.

Fig. 7.48. Four rings with surviving traces of fine cotton fabric from Burial 29.

But a more definite reason for the lack of textiles evidence from within the coffins was simply poor preservation for all textiles, heavy or light. As Miles and Connell (2012:54; see also Pearson et al 2011: 116) have stated in the context of the New Bunhills Burial Ground in London, 'consistent with other textile material recovered from 19th century burials, only the proteinic fibres of silk and wool remained. Cellulosic yarns such as linen and cotton decay in the presence of water and air within a short period and the complete absence of these fibres as cloth and stitching thread is thus usual.' The only observed examples of cellulose fibres at St. Johns were in a few cases where they had been preserved in contact with non-ferrous metals, and in the cases (described above) where some of the coffin covers had cotton weft and wool warp fibres (in all cases the cotton fibres were highly degraded). In addition, the conditions inside the coffins at St John's did not appear to favour textile preservation of either cellulose or protein fibres: the few fragments found clearly demonstrate that some clothes were once present, but simply have not survived.

8

Life and Death in Nineteenth Century Tokomairiro

The archaeological investigation of the St. Johns Cemetery can provide insights into the local nineteenth century settler community in two broad contexts: their way of life and their way of death. Bioarchaeological and historical evidence can provide information about the origins, wellbeing and lives of the settlers, and (in some cases) the ways they died. The archaeological evidence of their burial and coffins can then be used to consider their beliefs, cultural traditions and ways of dealing with death.

The Tokomairiro settlers buried at SJM in the 1870s were embedded in the mid-Victorian world, a world at once familiar and inexplicable to early 21st century eyes. Death was a Victorian obsession, particularly after the death of Prince Albert in 1861, when Queen Victoria entered a permanent period of mourning that lasted the rest of her life. But even before then the certainty of the Victorian era and its engineering and scientific advances were challenged by the inevitability of death, and often an early death. As Simon Schama (2002: 223) has stated:

'It (death) was all around them: in the typhus-riddled barracks of soldiers; in the cholera-infested slums of the poor; in the sputum-stained handkerchiefs of the tubercular middle classes.... The omnipresence of death seemed disproportionally chastening to a generation breezy with not entirely undeserved confidence that they had done more than any of their predecessors to master their physical environment. A civilisation that had made steam-driven ships float on the oceans, that had thrown great iron spans across broad rivers, and that had shrunk the world by electric telegraph must soon, surely conquer disease. It was indeed at this moment that advances in lensed microscopy were revealing, for the first time, the existence and culture of pathogens; although not (other than by use of the scrubbing brush) how their multiplication might be checked.

In this tantalizingly slight gap between knowledge and mastery, mortality entered to mock the Victorian sense of control over life. Perhaps the shock of translation from apparent omnipotent physical presence to the dumb inertia of death – the grievance of mortality – explains the extreme peculiarity of their rites of mourning; their determination to make the dead commandingly visible amidst the living. The immense scale and grandeur of Victorian tombs, with their passionate, hyperbolic masonry – so much more flamboyant than anything allowed for the living – are all attempts to postpone oblivion and absence.'

The settlers on the Tokomairiro Plains in the 1870s, who died and were buried at St. John's Cemetery, occupied a rapidly changing world. The adults had all been born overseas, in Britain and Europe, while many of the children were born in New Zealand (King et al 2021a). Some of the adults had gone to the Otago goldfields and then stayed on as the community settled down. Some aspects of this world were becoming 'modern': the railway connecting Milton to Dunedin had opened in 1875, the local newspaper (the *Bruce Herald*) had been established in 1865 and was published weekly, a telegraph office was opened in Milton in 1866 providing nationwide communications, and international telegraph contact between New Zealand and the world was established in 1876 when the first overseas telegraph cable came ashore. Horses still ruled the roads and farms, but the first mechanical road transport arrived in the 1860s when steam traction engines began to appear (Figure 8.1): the first mention of a local traction engine in the *Bruce Herald* was on 5 January 1870, when a machine won the machinery section at the Taieri Agricultural Show. The annual Tokomairiro Agricultural and Pastoral (A&P) show was established in 1866, and would have been visited by most of those buried at St. John's Cemetery, and is still held each year today (Figure 8.2, Figure 8.3).

However, as Schama points out above, medical science was only just emerging from the shadows. Milton's Bavarian-trained and Harley Street experienced doctor, Gustavus Weber, who is buried at St. Johns' Cemetery and is amongst the burials described here, could not save his own wife Flora (also included here) who died in childbirth in May 1874. The miasma theory of disease was only gradually being replaced by germ theory in the 1860s as a result of the work of Louis Pasteur and others, and there was no effective treatment for many diseases and infections. While patent medicines proliferated, promising (in a completely uncontrolled and unregulated fashion) all sorts of miracle cures, truly efficacious treatments were few and far between. But they were slowly appearing: for centuries the use of quinine to control malaria had been known (Rocco 2003), and smallpox vaccination was widely practiced from the eighteenth century onwards. In New Zealand the *Vaccination Act 1863* required each Provincial Superintendent to appoint medical officers to vaccinate against smallpox all people not already vaccinated who wished to do so, and required all children born after 1 March 1864 to be vaccinated. However, understanding of why these empirically derived treatments actually worked was still only developing.

And so all of the individuals who are described in this report were born into a world where the chances of an early death (often not even surviving childhood) were still staggeringly high by modern standards. This can be seen in the ages of the people studied here: 16 of the 27 individuals investigated at SJM were children and infants, a proportion unheard of in the 21st century western world. But a critical question for this study is whether or not these settlers were improving their lot: was life better in nineteenth century New Zealand than in the Old World countries that they had left behind? And probably more importantly to these people, were they bringing their children up in a world where their future life would be better than if they had stayed 'at home'? Infant and child mortality rates in the industrial towns and cities of Britain could reach as high as 246 deaths per thousand births (Huck 1995, Table 1), and so what was behind them was no bed of roses. Did they make the right decision?

Fig. 8.2. A medal awarded to James Drinnan at the 1886 Tokomairiro A&P Show (courtesy Dudley Finch). The annual show was established in 1866, and is still held annually. It is highly likely that the individuals that were investigated for this research attended the show in the 1870s, as we did during the excavations 150 years later.

Fig. 8.1. Harbinger of the modern world. Wayne Stevenson's 1886 McLaren traction engine (McLaren No. 221) that now resides near Waihola but spent its early working life in Southland. The 1860s saw the first appearance in the Tokomairiro area of steam-powered traction engines, which could haul loads on the road, pull ploughs and power machinery such as threshers and chaff cutters. This signalled the beginning of the end for horse and animal power, although it would be the internal combustion engine of the twentieth century that sealed this fate.

Fig. 8.3. Excavators from the SJM project Anna Willis, Teina Tutaki, Greg Hil and Baylee Smith at the 151st Tokomairiro A&P Show, 10th December 2016.

8.1. Life in Tokomairiro

The archaeological investigations at St John's Cemetery investigated 27 interments in 25 graves, Several detailed bioarchaeological biographies have been published on SJM individuals, including William Toogood (Burial 21), Joseph Higgins (Burial 11), Burial 13 and Burial 29 (Buckley at al 2020; Snoddy et al 2019; Snoddy et al 2021). Isotopic analysis has also been used to identify both diet and where several individuals came from, and importantly whether they were born locally (as it appears almost all of the infants and children were) or overseas (as all of the adults probably were) (King et al 2021a).

Here a slightly different perspective on the lives of two of these individuals is taken, incorporating different aspects of their social worlds and archaeological landscape. The life of Burial 11 (probably Joseph Higgins) is examined with particular regard to his career as a gold miner and his work, home and family at Canada Reef. This connects the community represented by the SJM individuals with

the important gold mining history of Otago. Secondly, the life of William Toogood (Burial 21) is examined, with particular focus on his membership of the Ancient Order of Foresters, and the important role that organisation had to play in early Milton. While both of these individuals are men, and numerous women were present at SJM, it is important to note that men are much easier to follow in historical records than women, and that both men left wives and families in precarious financial circumstances behind when they died. By looking at the lives and deaths of these two men, the tenuous existence of many women and children in the nineteenth century can also be addressed.

8.1.1. Joseph Higgins (Burial 11)

Burial 11 had a very well preserved skeleton that showed evidence of severe perimortem injuries (that almost certainly caused his death) as well as older, healed injuries. As described above the observed injuries match the contemporary newspaper accounts of the death of Joseph Higgins in an accident at Canada Reef in 1877, meaning that we are reasonably certain of his identification. Joseph Higgins was a gold miner, store keeper, family man and father, who died underground in a mine accident one Thursday evening in the late spring of 1877.

Joseph Higgins was born in late 1839 or early 1840 in Oxfordshire, England. His father, Mark Higgins farmed the 316 acre Menmarsh Farm at Stanton St. John, and employed 14 labourers, including a servant in the house. His mother, Sarah, was a local woman 26 years younger than her husband (1851 Census, Stanton St John, Oxfordshire, accessed on www.ancestrylibrary.com.au). Mark and Sarah had a large family of at least 11 children, of which Joseph was the eldest (a one year older brother, also Mark, was listed in the 1841 census but then disappears from the record, so presumably he died in infancy).

As the son of an established farmer it would be expected that Joseph would have had a reasonably comfortable childhood, but Mark Higgins was declared insolvent in 1855 (www.thegazette.co.uk), and so it is likely that the family went through periods of some hardship. The 1861 Census still shows the family to be at Menmarsh Farm, so presumably Mark Higgins was able to rebuild his finances. Joseph Higgins received an education, as the 1851 census (taken when he was 10 years old) lists him as a 'scholar' (meaning that he was attending school). But his infancy and childhood did have periods of ill health as linear enamel hypoplasia (LEH) on his teeth indicate numerous periods of physiological stress as the teeth formed (during his childhood). Given his background, it seems most likely that this evidence is due to childhood diseases rather than seasonal starvation. In a large family living in a single house it is likely that any illness would have circulated amongst all of the children. He had also fractured his left humerus (upper arm) when he was a child, which (as discussed further below) probably restricted its movement and left it partially numb.

The 1861 census lists him as a 'farmer's son' and still resident on Menmarsh Farm, and as the eldest surviving son it might be expected that he would take over the farm from his father, but Mark Higgins lived until 1887, ten years after Joseph's death (www.ancestrylibrary.com), so possibly Joseph saw no future there. Sometime in early 1861 Joseph and his brother Lawrence left Oxfordshire and travelled to New Zealand and continued to the Tuapeka goldfield soon after the start of the Gabriel's Gully rush, as on 3 September 1861 they each took out a Miner's Right at Tuapeka (Joseph No. 715 and Lawrence No.714), (www.kaelewis.com; Alexander Turnbull Library qms-2045). Their cousin Mark Higgins also came to New Zealand and opened a store at Waitahuna, and was involved in several mining ventures with Joseph (*Bruce Herald* 6 November 1872; Higgins Bankruptcy Trustee's Report, 1873, Archives New Zealand; Skinner 1947). The historical records for Joseph Higgins then draw a blank for nearly a decade, until he commenced business as a storekeeper at Canada Reef towards the end of 1870, and was closely associated with a number of mining ventures there until his death in one of the local mines in 1877.

Canada reef was a mining locality in the hills about 12km north-west of Milton, on the east side of the West Branch of the Tokomairiro River. This is rolling hill country, between 200 and 300 metres above sea level, and very exposed to weather coming from any direction. The Tokomairiro River runs in a deep valley through the hills, with the gold workings cut into the east side of the river valley and on the flatter ridges above. Today the Canada Reef area is a sheep farm, and consists of rolling pasture on the easier ground, with scrub in the gullies (Figure 8.4). The main indications of past occupation are clumps of old pine and macrocarpa trees that mark where miners' cottages once stood, and a few areas of old gold workings on the hillsides above the river. Until the 1970s this land was rough and scrubby, with old gold workings still open, but extensive farm

Fig. 8.4. Canada Reef in 2020. The landscape has changed considerably since the nineteenth century: farm development work in the 1970s and 1980s saw all of the more gently sloping land ploughed for pasture, and most of the old mine workings were filled in. Old macrocarpa and pine trees still mark where miner's houses and gardens once stood (right fore-ground and left mid-ground). The hills on the far side of the Tokomairiro River were planted in exotic forest in the 1970s (background).

development work in the 1970s and 1980s brought it into production, and many of the old workings and shafts were bulldozed. But enough archaeological evidence remains to still be able to consider the landscape that Joseph Higgins and his family occupied. An initial site survey in October 2020 identified a number of old occupation sites, mine workings and the site of one of the stamper batteries that crushed the ore from the local mines.

Mining began at Canada Reef in about 1866, continued through to the late 1870s, and then carried on intermittently until about 1908 (Marshall 1918). A number of different companies worked multiple claims on two main reefs that run 120 yards apart, the southern one called Canada Reef and the northern one Ocean View or Table Hill. As with all mining fields, the claim and company history is complex, as ventures were floated, failed, were restructured, and often failed again, sometimes several times over. Often the same people appear and reappear as shareholders in many different companies, and Joseph Higgins was no exception. From about 1870 until his death in 1877 he was a notable individual at Canada Reef as a miner and shareholder, and as a local storekeeper.

The first mining venture at Canada Reef was launched in 1866 when the Canada Quartz Reef Company was formed. It erected a 10 stamp battery, but the venture failed and the battery was sold for £1150 the following year at the insistence of the mortgagee. A new company, the Table Hill Quartz Mining Company was formed in 1867 by some of the shareholders of the earlier company, including Mark Higgins (but not at this date Joseph) (*Bruce Herald* 18

September 1867). It is also notable that William Bennetto (who would later become Joseph Higgins' father-in-law) was employed at the mine, and lived with his wife at Canada Reef (*Bruce Herald* 16 February 1870). In March 1870 15 tons of quartz were crushed for a return of only 3oz of gold, which was insufficient for the company to continue (*Bruce Herald* 9 March 1870). The mine and plant were then let on tribute (a system where a party works a mining claim, and pays a portion of any returns to the owner rather than a fixed rental or lease), but despite some reasonable returns at times once again this failed to pay sufficiently and the tributors abandoned the workings after 12 months (*Otago Daily Times* 21 March 1872).

Exactly when Joseph Higgins arrived at Canada Reef is not recorded, but he was definitely there by 1870. The Trustee's Report for his later bankruptcy (see below) stated that Joseph commenced business as a storekeeper at Canada Reef 'toward the end of the year 1870, without capital, being at that time the proprietor of one sixth share in a quartz claim' (Trustees Report, 1873, Archives New Zealand). This quartz claim was adjacent to the Table Hill QMC claim on a newly discovered reef, the Ocean View, which 'J. Higgins and party' were working (*Tuapeka Times* 14 September 1871). Joseph Higgins and several of the tributors from the previous venture had formed the Ocean View Company and applied for a ten acre claim (Section 16 Block V Table Hill) (*Tuapeka Times* 2 November 1871). They took over the old Canada Quartz Reef/Table Hill Quartz Mining Company battery (Figure 8.5, Figure 8.6), and began crushing stone from the new mine in September 1871 (*Otago Daily Times* 21 March

Fig. 8.5. Parts of the machinery of a quartz stamping battery. This was probably the mortar box of the original Canada Quartz Reef Company of 1866, which was later taken over by the Table Hill Company. It was driven by a 39 feet diameter water wheel. Joseph Higgins would been involved in the operation of this machinery in the early 1870s, when he was mining the Ocean View Reef.

1872). The first results were very encouraging, and other parties quickly took up a series of claims along the line of the reef and started to sink shafts (*Otago Daily Times* 21 March 1872). Some tension soon arose, as in late 1871 the Ocean View Company was subject to a claim jumping episode, and it was Joseph Higgins who fronted the legal challenge in November 1871. Dyer and party (who held the neighbouring claim) made an attempt to claim part of the Ocean View ground, and this led to a hearing where much of the legal argument revolved around minor details of how well the various claims had been pegged out (*Tuapeka Times* 16 November 1871).

Early enthusiasm on the new Ocean View line of reef soon died down, and a year later little work was being done. The Ocean View Company had protection over their claim, and were doing little, and the Alexandra Company, on the same line of reef, were planning a new shaft. Joseph Higgins had taken up on tribute part of the Table Hill Company's leased ground and had ten men working underground taking out stone (*Tuapeka Times* 10 October 1872). Occasional reasonable returns were reported, including a 40 oz cake of gold in November 1872 (*Bruce Herald* 20 November 1872). In November 1872 a new company, the Ocean View Quartz Mining Company, was formed to raise capital to sink a new shaft on the Ocean View claim. Joseph Higgins was one of the directors, along with his cousin Mark Higgins (*Bruce Herald* 6 November 1872).

But Joseph Higgins had over-extended himself, and the gamble had not paid off: his finances were unravelling,

and in April 1873 he was declared bankrupt (*Evening Star* 28 April 1873; *Otago Daily Times* 30 April 1873). The Trustees Report on his bankruptcy (Higgins, J. Trustees Report, Archives New Zealand) made it clear where the problems had arisen: he had started his business as a storekeeper at Canada reef in late 1870 with no capital, and supplied the men working the Ocean View claim with goods, a large proportion of which represented his contribution to the working expenses of the mine. The claim boundary dispute with Dyer and party in 1871 had added to Higgins' problems, and he estimated that he lost £200. Eight months of working the claim had cost £900, with his share of the gold recovered (he had to pay the claim owners 10% of the gross yield of gold) only being £320. Joseph's largest creditor was his cousin Mark Higgins to whom he owed £241 13s 8d. In order to address this Joseph had assigned to Mark his store and dwelling at Canada Reef, estimated to have cost £150, but Mark appears to have attempted to give Joseph no credit for the value of the buildings and the debt appeared in the schedule of creditors (Higgins, J. Trustees Report, Archives New Zealand). How this affected family relationships is not recorded.

After his bankruptcy Joseph Higgins stayed at Canada Reef, and continued to be involved in mining projects. There is no further record of what happened to his house and store that he had assigned to his cousin, but presumably he continued to live with his family in the house. In 1874 he applied for the agricultural lease of 143 acres (Section 28 Block III Table Hill District), so obviously was considering farming, but this application was withdrawn (*Tuapeka Times* 5 December 1874; 26 December 1874). Instead he carried on mining, and in May 1876 Joseph Higgins along with Mark Higgins, John Lanigan and Alexander Gillies applied for and were granted a prospecting claim on a new local reef. Ore crushings at the nearby Bruce Company's Battery gave encouraging if not spectacular results, but they lacked the capital to develop the mine (*Tuapeka Times* 31 May 1876; 23 August 1876), and by 1877 Joseph was working with a group of tributors in the Bruce Mining Company's workings at Canada Reef, which is where he died.

8.1.2. *Joseph Higgins' Home and Family Life*

While Joseph was involved in these mining operations as well as running his store, in 1871 he married Mary Ann Bennetto. Mary Ann was the daughter of William Bennetto, who had been employed by the Table Hill Quartz Mining Company and lived at Canada Reef. Mary Ann had been born in Cornwall in 1852, and travelled with her parents to the Victorian goldfields in Australia, where a brother and sister were born. By 1864 the family had moved to Otago, and another sister was born at Glenore in 1864 (www.ancestry.com). Presumably Mary Ann met Joseph Higgins at Canada Reef, and after their marriage they had three children there; Mark (born 1872), William (born 1874) and Sarah Jane (born 1875). Another son, Joseph, was born in May 1878 after Joseph's death.

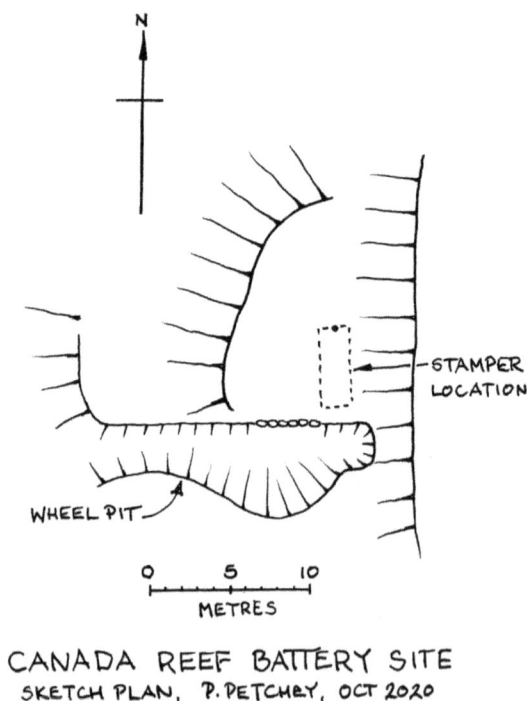

CANADA REEF BATTERY SITE
SKETCH PLAN, P. PETCHEY, OCT 2020

Fig. 8.6. Plan of the Canada Reef Battery site made during the initial archaeological site survey in October 2020 (Archaeological site H45/92).

By the early 1870s Joseph had suffered several injuries and ailments that would have had permanent effects. His childhood upper arm fracture probably restricted its movement and left the forearm partly numb, which may also explain the flattening of the tip of his left thumb, as the risk to this hand would have been increased. A healed rib fracture although temporarily debilitating would not have produced any long-term effects, but Joseph was certainly in constant discomfort from his teeth. He had lost a number of teeth due to decay, and his remaining teeth were crowded and many had massive caries. Infection from one tooth had spread into his right maxilla creating a massive alveolar lesion, and he also had severe periodontal disease. In addition, he smoked a pipe, and had worn pipe facts in his teeth where he clasped the pipe stem (Buckley et al 2020).

Joseph and Mary Ann's home was in the small mining community at Canada Reef, a settlement about which little is recorded. In 1875 there were eight men (and presumably their families) listed as being resident there, including Joseph Higgins and his father-in-law William Bennetto (Wises New Zealand Post Office Directory 1875-76), but newspaper accounts of various community events and activities suggest that the wider local population was much larger, if somewhat scattered. In 1872 the locals erected a community hall (suggesting that there were more than eight able-bodied men locally) and this hall was then used for dances and concerts as well as church services, performed occasionally by Rev. Arnott from Waitahuna (*Tuapeka Times* 10 October 1872). An *Otago Daily Times* correspondent who visited in 1872 commented that 'substantial houses for the workmen' were being built near the reef (*Otago Daily Times* 21 March 1872). The few surviving mining claim plans show a few scattered huts and cottages (Figure 8.7), indicating that Canada Reef was probably never a nucleated settlement, and the archaeological evidence supports this, with the scattering of house and hut sites marked by old macrocarpa and other exotic trees showing how spread out the community was (Figure 8.8). It is not known which one of these occupation sites was where Joseph and Mary Ann had a house and store, but the basic aspect of most identified occupation sites is similar, on flatter areas of the rolling countryside, particularly on a main spur where the reefs ran in a roughly east-west direction. Many of the houses would have been intervisible, meaning that despite the scattered nature of the community people would still be in regular sight and contact with their neighbours. Most people probably kept chickens and a few cows to feed their families, and Joseph Higgins was issued a depasturing licence for 5 head of cattle in October 1870 (*Tuapeka Times* 20 October 1870).

Local societies provided both social engagement and support, and records indicate that Mary Ann Higgins was engaged with the local community. She was a member

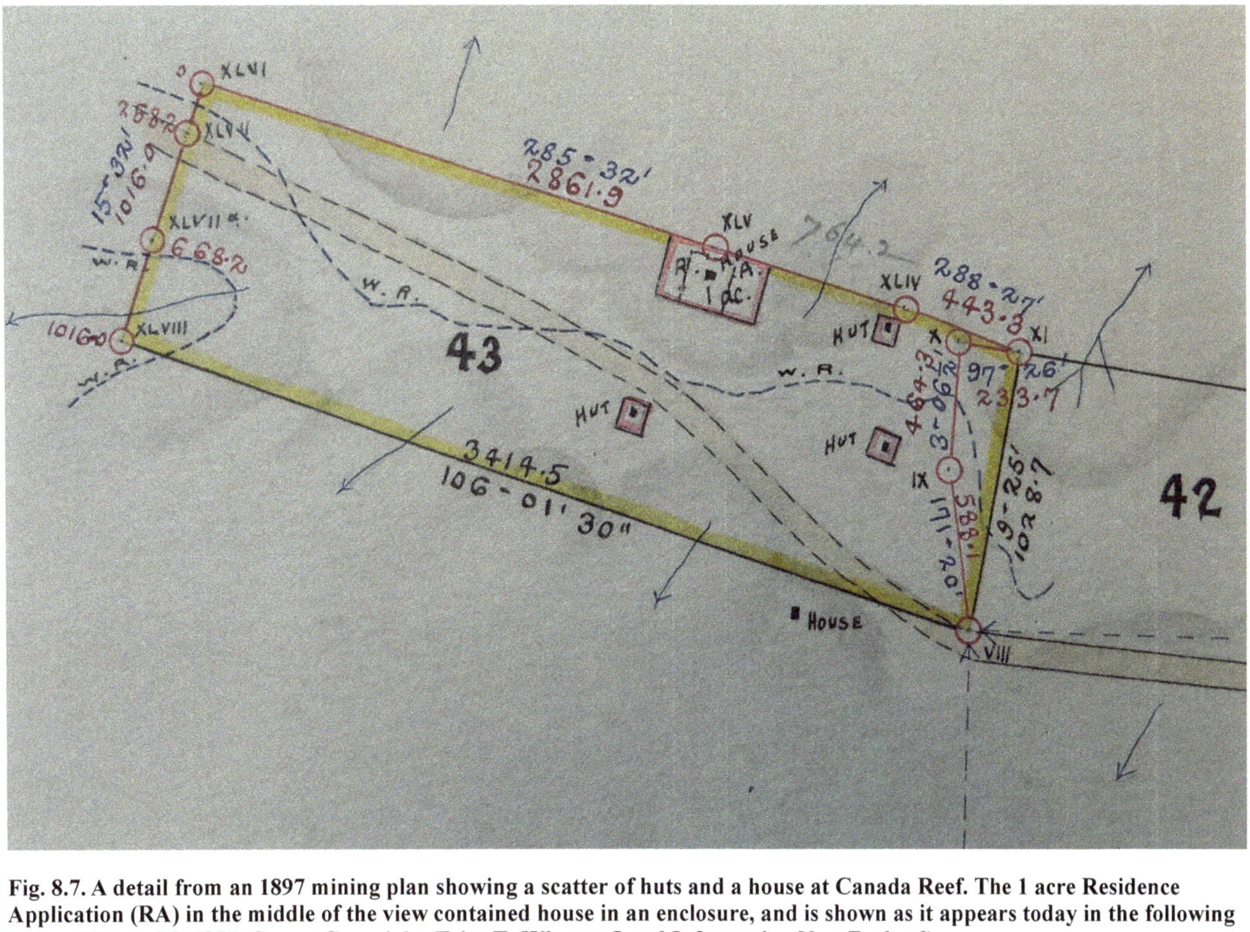

Fig. 8.7. A detail from an 1897 mining plan showing a scatter of huts and a house at Canada Reef. The 1 acre Residence Application (RA) in the middle of the view contained house in an enclosure, and is shown as it appears today in the following Figure (Otago SO 7357, Crown Copyright, Toitū Te Whenua Land Information New Zealand).

Fig. 8.8. The house site at Canada Reef shown in the previous Figure. The trees mark the site of a house on a one acre Residence Application, a form of legal tenure to allow for a miner to occupy an area of land for a house and garden. The system was administered by the Goldfields Wardens Courts.

of the Lodge Crystal Fountain of Canada Reef, No. 138 I.O.G.T. (Independent Order of Good Templars) which was formed in September 1876 (*Clutha Leader* 4 August 1876). The IOGT was a temperance movement that admitted both male and female members equally, and amongst the first elected officers was Jane Bennetto (Mary

Ann Higgins' mother). At a meeting a month later 'Sister' Higgins was also elected (*Bruce Herald* 14 November 1876). The Lodge met fortnightly in the public hall at Canada Reef. In October a concert and ball was held in Abel Kerr's barn (Figure 8.9) to celebrate the opening of the Lodge, which was attended by about 150 people, and

Fig. 8.9. The site of the farmstead at Abel Kerr's property at Canada Reef in 2021, now marked by a terrace and enclosure of trees (site H45/94). This is probably where the concert and ball was held in October 1876 to celebrate the establishment of the Lodge Crystal Fountain of Canada Reef, Independent Order of Good Templars.

the dancing continued until 4 or 5 in the morning (*Bruce Herald* 17 October 1876). Mary Ann Higgins was elected to the lodge in May 1877 ('Sis M.A. Higgins, W.L.H.S., for 'Worthy Left Hand Supporter') (*Bruce Herald* 18 May 1877). Joseph Higgins' name does not appear on any surviving records, so presumably he was not a member. Possibly he liked a drink or two but his wife disapproved? W. Dyer, with whom Higgins had had the expensive boundary claim dispute with in 1871, was elected District Deputy of District of Clutha of IOGT (*Clutha Leader* 16 November 1877). There were six lodges in the district: Hope of Balclutha, Star of Milton, Rose of Milburn, Crystal Fountain, Undaunted (Catlins River) and Home of Love (Clinton). Newspaper references to Lodge Crystal Fountain dry up after November 1878, and so it is likely that the Lodge went into abeyance at about that date.

8.1.3. *Joseph Higgins' Death*

Joseph Higgins last movements were recorded in detail during the inquest into his death, which took place at Canada reef on Saturday 10 November 1877, in front of E. H. Carew, the local coroner (*Bruce Herald* 13 November 1877). At about 2pm on the afternoon of Thursday 8 November 1877 Higgins and his father in law, William Bennetto, had walked to the Bruce Quartz Company's workings to start their shift. They were part of a group of nine men who had undertaken to extend one of the main levels (tunnels) of the mine for 100 feet in exchange for any gold recovered, with their wages topped up to £1 per week each if the gold fell short (*Bruce Herald* 13 November 1877). This suggests that returns were poor, and the men were working for meagre returns hoping for something better. The ground was a hard blue slatey rock and only a small amount of timbering was used to support the tunnels (Figure 8.10), partly because the miners thought that the rock was solid and secure, but also because of the poor returns and desire to dig quickly: good timbering cost time and money.

The main shaft of the mine measured 7 feet by 3 feet 6 inches (2.13m x 1.07m) and was 80 feet (24 metres) deep.

Fig. 8.10. An open adit at Canada Reef in 2020. This is one of the few remaining open tunnels at Canada reef: while not the drive where Joseph Higgins was killed, it shows the nature of the workings that he was in when the accident happened.

The shaft was equipped with winding equipment and ore buckets for raising stone, pipes for pumping water out of the mine, and a series of ladders down one side for the miners to descend and ascend (Hutton 1875). The stamping battery was close by, as the water turbine at the battery also powered the winding and pumping equipment (Hutton 1875).

Higgins and Bennetto would have walked past the shaft-head structures and no doubt greeted other men, before descending the ladders pausing only to light their lamps (electric mine lighting was still a decade away). They then walked along the 6 feet (1.83m) high tunnel for about 300 feet (90 metres), treading between the rails of the narrow gauge railway line laid along the floor of tunnel for the ore trucks. These small wagons were used to move rock from the mine face to the shaft, where it would then be hauled up to the surface for crushing (the gold bearing ore) or dumping (the waste rock, also called mullock, that contained no gold). The rock at the working face was broken up using explosives, and the loose rock then shovelled by hand into the trucks. At 8pm, after setting a charge and retreating to safety for the blast, the two men had got back to the working face with empty trucks and Bennetto went up to the face and started shovelling rock back. Behind him Higgins had just put two or three shovels of broken rock onto the truck when there was a crash, and a slab of rock from the roof fell down. A piece of rock struck Bennetto's arm, and he turned to find Higgins had been buried by the fall, with just part of his legs visible. Higgins let out a last groan. Bennetto could not hope to move the rock on his own, and ran back to the shaft to get assistance. He told several other miners what had happened and then ran to find Archibald Douglas, the local schoolmaster, who had some medical knowledge. In the meantime Harry McKenzie, Mitchell Park, Charles Todd (the mine manager) and one other man had gone down the mine, where they quickly pulled Higgins' body out from beneath the rock and carried him to the turning table, a flat sheet of iron where ore trucks were turned around, and laid him down. Archibald Douglas had by then descended the shaft and was able to examine Higgins: he felt no pulse, and when he cut a vein in Higgins' arm there was little bleeding. He placed a hand on Higgins' chest, and felt one last spasm of the heart. Douglas then pronounced Higgins dead.

From then on we can only speculate what happened. The men would have lifted Higgins' body up the shaft, and he would have been carried to his house nearby. Ahead of them William Bennetto would almost certainly have

Fig. 8.11. A mine shaft at Canada Reef in 2020. Most of the old workings have been filled in, but a few shafts and drives remain open: this one has been fenced off to prevent stock from falling in.

hurried to tell Mary Ann Higgins, his daughter, the bad news. She would have been distraught, not only at the sudden death of her husband, but also at the thought of being left with three young children, three months pregnant with a fourth, and in desperate financial circumstances. Higgins had insured his life for £100 with the Australian Mutual Provident Society only a year previously, but he had not paid his renewal premium and the policy had lapsed (*Evening Star* 12 November 1877).

Joseph Higgins' funeral was held at the St Johns Cemetery: he was buried in a wooden coffin covered in black fabric with a pressed iron coffin plate, embossed trim and plain cast iron handles. After the funeral a simple timber fence was constructed around the grave, but no headstone was ever erected. It was not an extravagant funeral, but neither does it appear to have been a pauper's funeral: someone paid for a respectable coffin and (presumably) service.

As Joseph Higgins' family had been left destitute by his death, the local community rallied to help, and several meetings were held to discuss ways of assisting Mary Ann Higgins. On Wednesday 21 November Alfred Jones, W. Dyer, R. Jones, R. Capstick and E. Marryatt met and discussed opening a subscription list for donations and staging a benefit concert to raise funds (*Bruce Herald* 23 November 1877). A further meeting at the Council Chambers in Milton was held on 26 November, with the Rev. Ronaldson in the chair, where more details of the concert were worked out (*Bruce Herald* 27 November 1877). The concert was held on 21 December 1877 at St. George's Hall in Milton, and 23 acts were staged (Figure 8.12). The subscription list was generously supported with donations received from 17 individuals, including £15 5s

CONCERT.

A CONCERT will be held at St. George's Hall, Milton,

By Amateur Performers, including the Christy Minstrels,

On FRIDAY next, 21st instant,

For the Benefit of the Widow and Children of the late Joseph Higgins.

Programme in next issue.

Gallery and front seats, 3s; back seats, 2s.

Doors open at 7.30, to commence at 8 o'clock p.m.

Fig. 8.12. The advertisement in the *Bruce Herald* (18 December 1877) for the benefit concert for Mary Ann Higgins and her children, who was left destitute after the death of Joseph Higgins (accessed on http://paperspast.natlib.govt.nz).

6d from Mark Higgins (*Bruce Herald* 26 April 1878). The concert and subscriptions together raised £95 11s, which after expenses provided £92 6s to Mary Ann. This was a considerable sum in 1878, but Mary Ann still faced an uncertain future as she had to raise three (soon to be four as her son Joseph arrived in May that year) young children herself.

Mary Ann Higgins stayed at Canada reef for a period, as her son was born there on 11 May 1878 (*Bruce Herald* 14 May 1878). After Joseph's death Mary remarried in 1884, to John Blackwood at Mataura, and died in 1887 in Timaru (www.ancestry.com). Joseph Higgins, the child born six months after his father's death, was listed in 1889 as having passed Standard IV at the Gore Public School, when he would have been 11 years old (*Mataura Ensign* 15 October 1889). He later moved to Clyde and Oamaru.

8.1.4. William Toogood (Burial 21)

William Toogood was born in 1830 (he was baptised on 27 June that year) to Titus and Mary Ann Toogood in Mitcham, London. His father was an agricultural labourer (Baptism Register, St. Peter and St. Paul, Mitcham, 1813-1833; 1841 England Census: Access through www.ancestrylibrary.co.au). His was a very large family, with records indicating that he had 14 siblings. They were certainly poor, with a large family living off a labourer's wages, and modern analysis of William's teeth identified numerous occurrences of LEH that indicate several periods of physiological stress (infection or malnutrition) during childhood (Buckley et al 2020; Snoddy et al 2019). In 1843 William, his parents and several siblings departed on the *King William* for Hobart, Tasmania, where at least two more brothers were born.

In 1857 William married Elizabeth Ann Smith in Hobart. Elizabeth Ann had been born in Redhill in Surrey in about 1837, but there is no record of when she came to Tasmania. Her obituary stated that she married William in 1855 and came to Hobart the following year (*Bruce Herald* 28 August 1919), but this does not match other records that place William in Hobart twelve years earlier, and their marriage was registered in Hobart in May 1857 (www.ancestry.com, Australia Marriage Index 1788-1950). William and Elizabeth Ann would eventually have 11 children (*Bruce Herald* 28 August 1919), of whom four boys were born in Hobart (William, Richard, Henry and a male child who probably died at birth or in infancy as there are no further records of him).

In 1861 William moved to New Zealand to take part in the Gabriel's Gully rush, and Elizabeth and the children followed in 1862 after which the family settled at Helensbrook (*Bruce Herald* 28 August 1919). Helensbrook is now a suburb at the northern end of Milton, but then it was a rural locality beside the main road north of the township, notable as the location of the Police Camp as well as the showgrounds where the annual A&P show is still held. It is likely that William and Elizabeth Ann rented a house there for several years, but in 1869 William purchased a ½ acre property for £100 (Otago Deeds 26/930). This small piece of land would probably have provided the Toogood family with space to grow vegetables, keep chickens and possibly even a cow. They lived in a small cottage that faced the main south road leading into Milton. No images of the cottage are known, but it was shown on a 1909 plan (Figure 8.13). The ½ acre property still exists at 341 Union Street (SH1) Milton, but the cottage was replaced by a new house probably in the 1920s (Figure 8.14).

William worked as a labourer, and his death certificate also listed butcher and forestry. His father was an agricultural labourer, so possibly he followed a similar path, as an itinerant labourer doing whatever came to hand. Certainly he would not have been highly paid, and he had a growing family to care for and feed. However, he was clearly financially prudent. He held four shares in the

Bruce Property Investment and Building Society, which enabled him to raise a 100% mortgage with that society to purchase his Helensbrook property (Otago Deeds 23/923), and he was also a member of (and advocate for) the Court Bruce of the Ancient Order of Foresters (AOF). This was one of a number of nineteenth century 'friendly societies' that provided a form of social insurance for its members in a period before social welfare support was provided by government (which would not happen until the 1930s) (Carlyon 2001; Olssen 1996). William Toogood was a regular attendee at the meetings held initially at the White Horse Hotel, and later at various locations around Milton (*Bruce Herald* 11 February 1873; Sumpter and Lewis 1949: 159). The friendly societies and their role in Milton are discussed in more detail below.

However, although William appears to have got his family life on a firm footing, at the age of just 42 he fell seriously

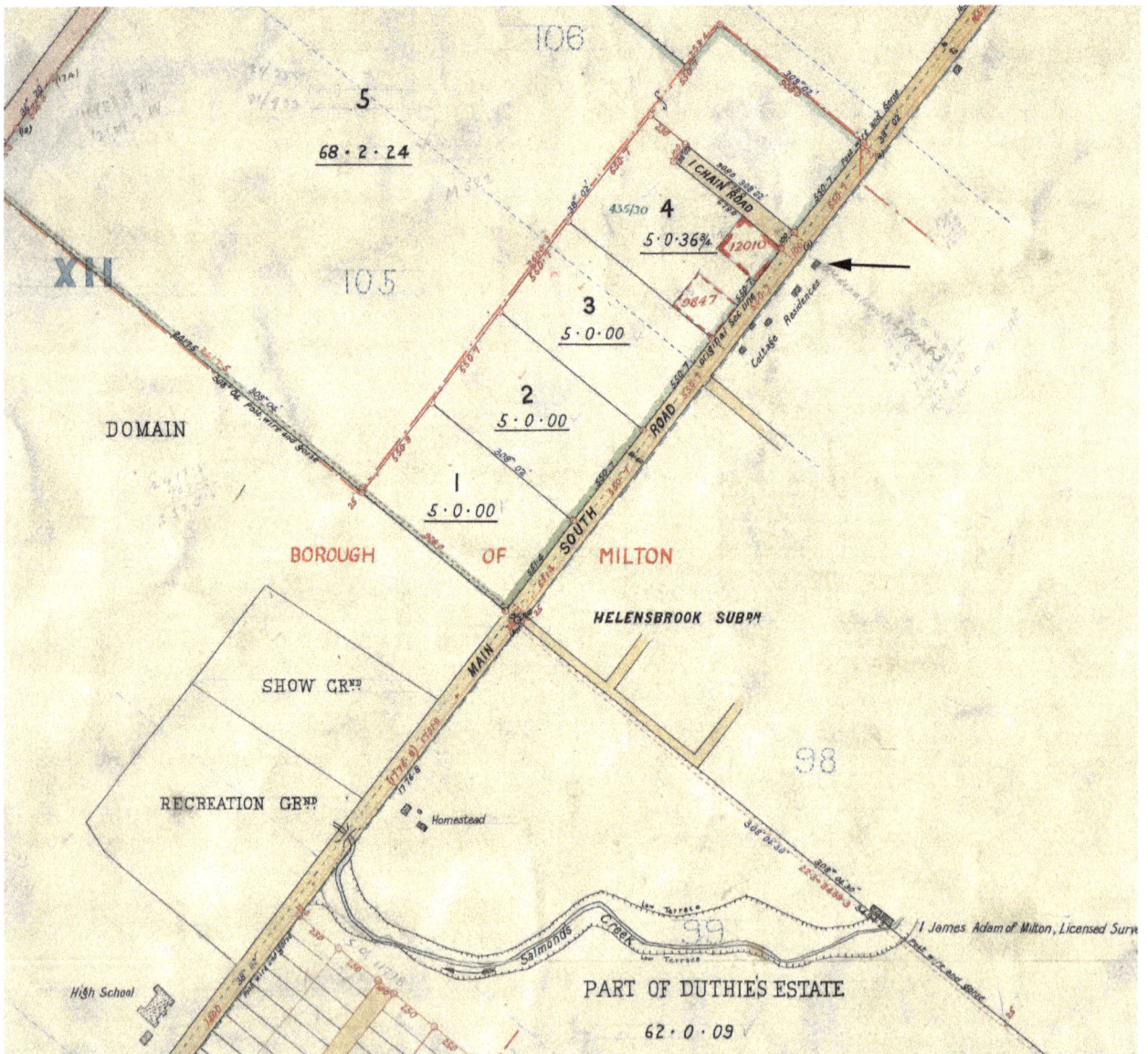

Fig. 8.13. A detail from a 1909 plan, showing the Helensbrook area at the north end of Milton. The cottage that was William Toogood's is indicated by the arrow (Otago Deeds Plan 309, Crown Copyright, Toitū Te Whenua Land Information New Zealand).

76

Fig. 8.14. The house that now stands at 341 Union Street (State Highway 1) at Helensbrook just north of Milton. William Toogood bought this ½ acre property in 1869, and he died here in 1873. His cottage was replaced by the present house in the early twentieth century.

ill with that Victorian scourge, tuberculosis (diagnosed as *pneumonic pthsisis haemorrhage* on his death certificate), although it is likely that he had been infected years earlier as the infection can lie dormant for long periods (Snoddy et al. 2019). In about March or April 1872 William became incapacitated and was unable to work and support his family. Analysis of his remains in 2019 showed that in addition to the pulmonary tuberculosis that would have been obvious at the time as his lung function declined, he also suffered from disseminated secondary tuberculosis resulting in severe skeletal lesions, with particular damage to the left femur and hip, which probably made any movement painful (Snoddy et al 2019). Adding to his discomfort would have been his very poor dental health, with pipe facets worn from pipe smoking, periodontal disease and severe caries; the entire crown had been destroyed on two teeth, and six teeth had been lost antemortem (Buckley at al 2020; Snoddy et al 2019). As William's health declined through 1872 he would have required more and more care from his family, with the burden almost certainly falling on Mary Ann, although the older children would likely have helped. At some stage he would have had required assistance with mobility, hygiene, and feeding, possibly including special preparation of high calorie, easily digested foods. Nineteenth century western medicine often prescribed opiates such as laudanum to manage the pertussis from pulmonary TB, and these drugs are themselves associated with their own functional impacts such as cognitive impairment and respiratory depression (Snoddy et al 2019).

William's membership of the AOF paid off, as he was financially supported by the organisation for the final 11 months of his life, until he died in early February 1873. This support was a payment of £1 for the first 26 weeks, which was then reduced to 10 shillings a week for the subsequent period (Ancient Order of Foresters 1898). During this period William would have been visited weekly by the Court Woodward (one of the formal positions in each lodge) who would ensure that he was still too sick to work and would have made the weekly payment. The AOF then also paid for his funeral, £20 being the standard payment (Ancient Order of Foresters 1898; *Otago Daily Times* 6 August 1870). The 7 February 1873 edition of the *Bruce Herald* contained both the funeral notice (placed by the undertaker, J. Wallace), and also a notice from the AOF that members were requested to meet to attend the funeral of 'Brother Toogood,' wearing their neck ribbons and white gloves.

Given the pomp and ceremony beloved of all of the friendly societies, including the AOF, and the requirement for members to wear regalia, it is likely that the funeral was a large and formal affair. It was organised by local undertaker James Wallace, who advertised that he had a 'hearse, plain or mounted, for one or two horses' for hire (*Bruce Herald* 30 June 1869). William's coffin was adorned in typical fashion for the period, with black cloth cover, embossed metal trim, coffin plates and cast iron handles, but also appears to have had an ornate painted decoration on the lid. Not enough of this survived to determine the nature of the design, but it may have been similar to the AOF crest reproduced on sashes and other regalia. The AOF members, in their regalia, would have followed the hearse bearing the coffin from William's property on the main road around to the cemetery on Back Road, where the Church of England burial service would have been performed.

Mary Ann Toogood and her surviving children (six children at the time between the ages of 5 and 16, although the oldest was probably already working) were left in a house with a debt still owed to the building society. The AOF had a District Relief Fund that was intended to provide support for the widows and families of deceased members, and Mary Ann was assisted from that (although the amount was not recorded) (*Otago Daily Times* 6 August 1870). Local AOF members also raised a further £17 from the local community to help pay some of the building society loan (*Bruce Herald* 10 October 1873). Mary Ann finally paid off the mortgage in 1877, by which time it stood at £41 (Otago Deeds 64/39). She continued to live at the house, and in 1892 transferred ownership to her son Henry Oscar Toogood (Otago Deeds 100/223). Mary Ann was probably illiterate (the Deed documents are signed by a cross and the note 'her mark'), and so she has left no written records, and documents of the period simply identify her as a 'widow.' It is therefore not possible to determine how she supported herself and her family after William's death, but even with the support of her older children it would have been a tough life. But according to her obituary she remained in good health until her eyesight failed when she was about 78 (*Bruce Herald* 28 August 1919).

Mary Ann never remarried, and died aged 82 years in 1919 at the home of her daughter and son-in-law, Campbell Cowie (*Bruce Herald* 28 August 1919). She was buried at the Fairfax Cemetery, as by this date interments in the old St. Johns Cemetery, where William had been buried, had ceased.

8.2. Care and the Community

The case studies of Joseph Higgins and William Toogood and their families illustrate a number of themes regarding both individuals and the community in nineteenth century Tokomairiro. Both men came from an agricultural background in Britain, although of slightly different socio-economic status; Joseph Higgins was the son of a farmer and William Toogood was the son of an agricultural

labourer. But on coming to New Zealand both participated in the Gabriels Gully gold rush, and both engaged in manual labour for a living. Arguably William, from the poorer background, fared better in New Zealand as he owned a small freehold property, while Joseph suffered a series of failures in his mining speculations and was declared bankrupt at one stage. Both men married and had large families, but tragedy and an early death struck both of them. Both left a wife and children behind in difficult financial circumstances when they died. This was not deliberate neglect, but instead illustrates how tenuous many peoples' existences were in nineteenth century New Zealand (and almost everywhere else). The death or desertion of a breadwinner could leave a family destitute. But there were mechanisms to protect against this eventuality, very much founded in a synthesis of the late Victorian ideologies of self-help and mutualism. Although there was no state social welfare system (that would appear in the 1930s), the 'migrants from a society in which a pauper's funeral constituted the ultimate terror' (Olssen 1996: 180) developed their own protections against the risks of sickness, destitution and an anonymous death.

8.2.1. The Ancient Order of Foresters and other Community Organisations

Joseph Higgins had taken out a commercial £100 life insurance policy, but had failed to pay the premium and his family therefore failed to receive this benefit, while William Toogood had joined the Ancient Order of Foresters (AOF), and he and his family were supported by that organisation. The Ancient Order of Foresters was one of a number of 'friendly societies' that were established in the nineteenth century, predominantly in England but then transported by migrants to the New World. These societies acted as a source of community security and identity through regular meetings and social events, and as private insurance providers, as membership required the payment of a regular fee for which the member received cover in case of incapacity to work due to illness or injury and for medical and funeral expenses. The societies active in New Zealand included the Ancient Order of Foresters, the Manchester Unity Independent Order of Oddfellows, the Independent Order of Oddfellows (a breakaway group from the Manchester Unity), the Hibernian Australasian Catholic Benefit Society, and the united Ancient Order of Druids, of which the Manchester Unity and AOF were to become the largest in the country (*Appendices to the Journals of the House of Representatives* 1881, H-7: 2; Olssen 1996: 178).

The friendly society movement was introduced to Dunedin within the first year of settlement, when the Hand and Heart Lodge of the Manchester Unity Independent Order of Oddfellows was formed in December 1848 (Dougherty 2017: 112). In Milton, the Court Bruce of the AOF was established in 1865, and was the first such society in the area. For a regular weekly contribution of one shilling members were eligible for the free services of the Court surgeon (in this case, Dr. Weber) and provision of medicines, £1 per week financial support should they be unable to work, and £20 paid towards funeral expenses in case of death (Ancient Order of Foresters 1898; *Bruce Herald* 10 August 1865; 14 August 1872; Carlyon, 2001; Sumpter and Lewis 1949: 159). Some idea of the support provided by the AOF in Milton can be gained from their published expenses for the August 1875 to August 1876 year (*Bruce Herald* 24 February 1876):

Paid -	For sick pay	£38 19 6
	Doctor and chemist	£178 10 6
	District levy	£21 18 6
	Funeral donations	£40 0 0
		£279 8 6

It can be seen from this that their greatest support was in providing access to medical care, but that funeral expenses were a not insubstantial secondary expense (£40 expenditure suggests that two funerals were paid for that year). The records of the Court Bruce do not appear to have survived, so there is no record of membership other than newspaper accounts, but it is notable that three of the individuals encountered during the 2016 investigation were associated with the organisation: William Toogood (member, assisted during sickness); Henry Pim (member and secretary); and Dr Gustavus Weber (Surgeon).

In this early period the friendly societies also served an important role in community building. In scattered isolated embryonic communities the societies combined the benefits of mutuality with social activity and acted as agents of social integration: in the early years of settlement people joined as much for the social life as for the welfare benefits (Carlyon 2001: 247; Olssen 1996: 181). And it was not just the friendly societies that performed this role: many organisations operated ostensibly with one purpose but also created social contacts and social cohesion: examples here being Mary Ann Higgins' membership of the Lodge Crystal Fountain, Independent Order of Good Templars (a temperance movement) and Robert Rowley Thomson's membership of the No. 2 Battalion of the Otago Rifles (a volunteer military organisation). Regular meetings of these organisations, together with social events (such as the concert and ball held for the opening of the Lodge Crystal Fountain) ensured social contact and unity. One aspect of many of these societies, including the AOF, was pomp and ceremony: the funeral of William Toogood was attended by members of Court Bruce of the AOF who were requested to attend in 'neck ribbons and white gloves' (Figure 8.15) (*Bruce Herald* 7 February 1873), while Robert Rowley Thomson was buried with full military honours, including three rifle volleys fired over the grave (*Bruce Herald* 11 September 1877).

The evidence of the efficacy of these organisations to provide social support and cohesion can be demonstrated in the evidence from the St. John's Cemetery. As both of the above detailed case studies illustrate, wider community mechanisms were at play, filling the void left for Joseph

Fig. 8.15. A detail of an Ancient Order of Foresters ceremonial sash. This would have been worn at AOF meetings and events.

Higgins' family after his failure to pay his life insurance premiums, and also helping William Toogood's family beyond the simple benefits due from AOF membership. The benefit concert staged to raise funds for Mary Ann Higgins was not held by any one society or group, but was organised by members of the community including W.J. Dyer, who was District Deputy of District of Clutha of the Independent Order of Good Templars (of which Mary Ann was a member) (*Clutha Leader* 16 November 1877), while one of the largest benefactors was local landowner Abel Kerr in whose barn the concert and ball to celebrate the opening of the lodge had been held (*Bruce Herald* 26 April 1878). But also notable was that W.J. Dyer was also the leader of the mining party taken to court by Joseph Higgins in 1871 over a claim dispute, the costs of which contributed to Higgins' bankruptcy. Clearly nineteenth century social relations were as complex and convoluted as in the modern world.

Table 8.1 shows the identified individuals from the St. John's Cemetery investigations, the local organisations that they (or their spouse) belonged to, and the direct and indirect effects that can be attributed to these associations.

The discussion so far has focussed on the individuals buried in the St. John's Cemetery who can be reasonably confidently identified, and their stories can therefore be woven together using both archaeological and historical evidence to produce a confident narrative. But most of the people investigated in 2016 cannot be identified by name: nevertheless it is possible to consider their wellbeing and especially their support within the community. The 'bioarchaeology of care' is an approach whereby archaeological evidence of community care of disabled, ill or injured individuals is studied in order to examine past behaviours and communities; archaeological evidence of past care can indicate a socially stable and cohesive society experienced in nursing the sick (Tilley 2015; Tilley and Oxenham 2011). This approach can be applied to St. John's Milton individuals in the knowledge (based on the above discussion) that the local community did have mechanisms to care for at least some of those in need.

For many illnesses and injuries only the soft tissues would be affected, and so nothing will remain in the archaeological record, but traumatic injuries causing bone fractures are detectable (as in the case of Joseph Higgins who suffered major trauma) while long-term illness can also affect bone (as in the case of William Toogood's tuberculosis). Burial 13, an adult male, had three healed rib fractures, although

it is not possible to say exactly when these occurred, plus a possible healed plastic deformation fracture to the right femur that would have occurred during childhood (Buckley et al 2020). Minor traumatic injuries were common in this period (horses and livestock accidents being particularly prevalent), and are likely to have prevented an individual from working for several weeks.

Burial 29 was a young-middle aged adult (20-34 years) female whose remains showed distinct abnormalities and some distinct differences in terms of lifetime health compared to the others interred at St. Johns Cemetery (Buckley et al 2020; King et al 2020; Snoddy et al 2021). She was buried in one of the more ornate (and therefore expensive) coffins found during the 2016 excavation: it was fitted with a large coffin plate, embossed trim and eight cast iron handles. This would appear to place her in the middle to upper level of affluence of those interred at St. Johns, although the lack of a headstone possibly discounts a higher level of wealth.

Results of isotopic analysis are consistent with her origin in the United Kingdom, and she was probably weaned at an early age, prior to nine months old (King et al 2020). Her teeth had no linear enamel hypoplasia (LEH), the only individual at SJM without this evidence of childhood growth disturbance, suggesting that she had a childhood that was protected from periods of hunger and/or illness that all of the others experienced. Isotopic analysis also suggests that she maintained a relatively consistent diet, with high meat content, from childhood though to her death as an adult, including the period of her immigration to New Zealand (King et al 2020). However, her remains showed clear evidence of some form of severe skeletal dysplasia (an inherited growth disorder). She probably had a severe underbite, which may have affected her speech. She showed distinct bilateral asymmetry, with her left side muscle and ligament attachments noticeably more robust than on the right. Her ribs were asymmetric, with the left ribs having a pronounced flattening and superior curvature of the shafts, her spine was probably curved, and her upper limbs were disproportionately shorter than her lower

Table 8.1. Individual's membership of community organisations.

Name	Date of death	Organisation	Direct influence/effect	Indirect influence
Henry Pim	1872	Court Bruce, Ancient Order of Foresters (secretary)		
William Toogood	1873	Court Bruce, Ancient Order of Foresters	Financial support while ill. Funeral expenses paid. Allowance to widow.	Members of AOF raised further £17 to contribute towards payment of mortgage.
Gustavus Adolphus Weber	1874	Surgeon to Court Bruce Ancient Order of Foresters		
Robert Rowley Thomson	1877	No. 2 Battalion of the Otago Rifles	Buried with full military honours	
Joseph Higgins	1877	Wife (Mary Ann) member of Lodge Crystal Fountain, Independent Order of Good Templars	Unknown, but funeral expenses were paid and fence erected around the grave by someone.	Lodge members involved in organising concert to raise funds for Mary Ann (£92 6s).

limbs. The joints in her hands and feet had clear areas of active resorption, as did her left knee. Her teeth showed very little wear, although this was possibly due to her jaw misalignment preventing the teeth from aligning correctly, but she had severe periodontal disease. She was also the only adult investigated at St Johns Cemetery that did not have pipe facets in her teeth. In addition, there appears to have been a perimortem (i.e. at about the time of death) sharp force injury on the sternum.

Overall it is clear that Burial 29 had suffered from some form of skeletal dysplasia from childhood, probably an inherited connective tissue disorder. It would have left her with some mobility issues, possibly some difficulties in using her left arm and pain in her hands and feet. She would also have appeared different to her peers, with a twisted torso, possible hunchback from scoliosis and/ or a raised shoulder, prominent gapped teeth, a possible underbite and bowed legs (Snoddy et al 2021). In colonial New Zealand any form of disability would have been a major disadvantage, as most settlers would have been expected to work, especially as domestic servants were in short supply so even middle-class women were expected to do more than they would in the United Kingdom. Official efforts were made to restrict the immigration of people seen as unable to contribute to society, the *Imbecile Passengers Act* 1882 being one such attempt (Snoddy et al 2021). And yet Burial 29 with her obvious disabilities had come to New Zealand, and appears to have enjoyed a consistent diet all of her life with no evidence of the periodic stress during childhood that all other individuals at St. Johns Cemetery displayed. Her dietary life history and relatively elaborate coffin furniture suggest that she may have been born into a family with greater wealth than others in the community (King et al. 2020), protecting her from the vicissitudes of fortune that afflicted many of her neighbours.

Whatever the reality of her situation, it is clear that Burial 29 received care from infancy onward, and while she may not have required community assistance of the kind showed to the Higgins and Toogood families, she would have been part of the community. Her death and burial were marked in the same way as others, with a coffin decorated in the style of the period and presumably a funeral conducted in the same way as others buried in the same cemetery.

8.3. Death and Funerals in Tokomairiro

The previous section dealt with the living, their care, and the role of the community and community organisations. But once an individual died, their funeral was the last community engagement with that person. As Simon Schama (2002) is quoted above as stating, the Victorians were notable for the extreme peculiarity of their rites of mourning, and the most tangible archaeological evidence for these rites are the monumental headstones found in most Victorian cemeteries in the Anglo-world. These have been the subject of much academic study, but the present research focuses solely on unmarked and unidentified

graves, meaning that it is the coffins that provide archaeological evidence for funerary traditions.

The descriptions of the coffins and coffin furniture given above show that all of the St. John's Cemetery burials that were investigated fit within the same funerary tradition, with timber coffins covered with dark (usually black) fabric and trimmed with embossed metal strips, coffin plates and cast-iron handles. Variation is mainly limited to the quantity and quality of such furniture, with coffin handles most likely to be omitted. Most of these burials were interred in the 1870s, and comparison with archaeological literature from the UK and New Zealand indicates that the St. Johns coffins were consistent with the widespread funerary traditions in the Anglo-world in this period (and well into the 1890s). The major difference observed in the present research, which includes the goldfields cemeteries of Lawrence and Drybread and Cromwell (Petchey et al 2018; Petchey, Buckley and Scott 2018; reports in preparation), is that 'frontier' cemeteries tended to contain plain wooden coffins with little or no decoration while burials of more 'settled' times and places conformed to the traditions of the day. Circumstance trumped tradition on the goldfields frontier, but in the settled agricultural community of Milton the undertaker was undoubtedly busy making and decorating coffins.

As Hoile (2018: 218) has pointed out funeral directors supplied the coffins and coffin furniture at a considerable profit margin, so part of any variation in coffin furnishing was almost certainly directly associated with the cost of the coffin (and therefore by extension the overall funeral), and can therefore tentatively be related to the socio-economic status of the interred individuals. That this is tentative, and needs to be applied cautiously as an easy explanation for all variation, is illustrated by William Toogood's (Burial 21) coffin. This coffin had a coffin plate, embossed trim and simple handles, but as described above he could not work for the last 11 months of his life was supported by Ancient Order of Foresters who also paid for the funeral. Therefore, he could be considered poor, but other mechanisms (the AOF) were at play to ensure a 'respectable' burial.

What counted as a respectable or fashionable funeral is of some interest in this period. The use of overtly decorative elements in coffin furnishing fits within the 'Beautification of Death' movement of the nineteenth century, whereby funerals could involve considerable ostentatious rites and ornamentation, and also is consistent with funerary traditions in other parts of the British Empire and Anglo-world (Cowie et al 2008; Hoile 2018; Mahoney-Swales et al 2011: 219, 221; Miles and Connell 2012; Pearson et al 2011). A counter to the Beautification of Death movement was the Funeral Reform movement that advocated for simpler funerals that did not place such a financial burden on the bereaved (Fraser 2012: 101). This debate was present in New Zealand, as it was discussed in newspaper articles of the time (e.g. *Bruce Herald* 15 June 1875; *Otago Witness* 21 November 1874). One newspaper report is worth quoting here, as it both describes the reform approach as well as the more standard coffin treatment:

The remains of the Mr Stuart Hawthorne, late rector of the High School, were interred in the North Dunedin Cemetery on Friday last. As showing that the funeral reform is making some advance in Dunedin, it may be mentioned that no palls, scarfs, or mourning coaches were used, while the coffin was of plain cedar, without the usual covering of black cloth, with a large cross of blackwood upon it (Bruce Herald 15 June 1875).

Funerals could be very expensive. In 1866 the contract price from Spicer and Murray to the Otago Provincial Council for undertaking any funerals as required by the government was £25, which included the minister, interment fees, conveyance and all charges (but with a 2s extra charge for every mile beyond 3 miles of Dunedin) (*Otago Provincial Government Gazette*, Vol. X No. 457, 31 December 1866). The standard amount the AOF made available to pay for the funerals of members was £20, which was enough to pay for a perfectly respectable funeral.

In Milton, as in many other places in contemporary New Zealand, the coffins were probably made by a local carpenter or joiner. In 1866 J. Hollick of the Tokomairiro Timber Yard was advertising 'Funerals Furnished' as well as building materials of every description, a large quantity of bricks and glass cut to any size (*Bruce Herald* 29 November 1866). In 1869 James Wallace appears to have set up business more specifically as an undertaker, and advertised that he was 'now prepared to execute funerals to suit the requirements of all parties,' with a hearse for hire (Figure 8.16) (*Bruce Herald* 30 June 1869). As described above, it was Wallace who buried William Toogood. Wallace continued in business until 1876, when after his own death his widow advertised the funeral hearse for sale by tender (*Bruce Herald* 20 June 1876). It is likely that it was James Wallace who advised on, supplied, and then was paid for, the fashionable funerals of which the coffins recorded in 2016 are now the only surviving tangible evidence. He probably sourced the timber for the coffins

and the coffin cloth to cover them locally, but the coffin plates (depositum plates), handles (grips) and embossed metal ribbon (coffin lace) were all mass-produced in the United Kingdom (particularly Birmingham) and exported for the vast and profitable trade in funerals. The presence of all of these items at St. Johns Cemetery ties Milton in with the economy, fashion and cultural traditions of the late nineteenth century Anglo-world.

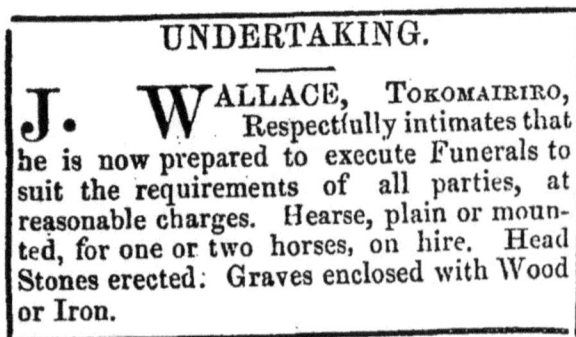

Fig. 8.16. James Wallace's advertisement in the *Bruce Herald* of 30 June 1869 (accessed on http://paperspast. natlib.govt.nz).

9

Conclusions

The excavations at St. John's Church of England Cemetery in 2016 investigated the remains of 27 individuals, most of who probably died in the 1870s. Over half were infants and children, a terrifying death rate amongst the young by modern standards. Amongst the adults appalling oral hygiene was almost ubiquitous, with tooth loss, caries and periodontal disease rife. Examination of teeth also revealed multiple occurrences of linear enamel hypoplasia (LEH) in every individual except one, indicating that all (except that one) suffered periods of physiological stress in childhood from illness and/or hunger. This applied whether the individual had grown up in Britain (or Europe) or in Milton. Death from tuberculosis; the 'sputum-stained handkerchiefs of the tubercular middle classes' (Schama 2002); was still common as many of these first generation of settlers had unknowingly brought the dormant infection with them, only for it to take a grip on its victims in their new home.

Not only did the settlers' health reflect their origins, but they also brought many of their funeral traditions with them; the archaeological evidence of the St John's Cemetery burials are consistent with other European settler burials of the same period elsewhere in New Zealand and in the Anglo-world. The small rural churchyard graveyard setting was consistent with traditional British practice (although this has already largely passed in the UK) (Deed 2015), the same coffin motifs and decorations could be found in London and Milton (and those found in Milton had almost certainly been manufactured in Birmingham). And the settlers had also imported their mechanisms for survival in a challenging and uncertain world; in particular the friendly societies with their ceremonies, social events and insurance against a pauper's burial.

Therefore at first glance it appears that the answer to the question of whether the people's lives were 'better' in the colony than back in Britain or Europe is that there had been no improvement. The archaeological and bioarchaeological study of this Victorian-era population sample suggests that the colonial society transported their biosocial landscape on immigration and little changed for these initial colonists (Buckley et al. 2020). But this does not necessarily account for the new world that they were creating for their children and grandchildren.

As Holland (2013) has explored, it took time for the new settlers to learn about their new home. The promises of a better life that had attracted many to the colonies (Figure 1.1) were not to be immediately realised for many; the mild mid-latitude climate and rich soils were not quite as promised, and it took time to carve farms out of virgin bush, tussock-covered hills or flax-covered swamp. The first generation of yeoman settlers had to acquire land, break it in, develop their farms and build up their herds. While they were doing so life was not going to be easy, and medical science was only on the verge of new discoveries (notably the emergence of germ theory) that could save the lives of them and their children.

But some things were improving. William Toogood, the son of an agricultural labourer who could probably have never owned land in Britain owned a ½ acre and cottage that would have provided him and his children with shelter and food. His early death from tuberculosis in 1873 left his family in desperate circumstances, but by 1877 his widow had paid off the debt owing on the property. All of the burials in the cemetery conformed with the funerary traditions of the time: there were no obvious 'paupers burials' found. While it could be argued that this is evidence of people feeling under social pressure to conform and spend money on expensive funerals (the point of the Funeral Reform Movement), it can also be argued that everyone in the community was at least afforded a decent burial. Certainly at 'home' in London and other large cities in this period the dead had often buried in overfull cemeteries, sometimes with multiple coffins in a single grave, and with a high likelihood that they would be disturbed by new grave excavations within a year or two. In the new New Zealand cemeteries the dead were afforded more dignity.

Overall the excavations at St. John's Cemetery investigated a first generation settler population that was of predominantly (but not exclusively) British origin, with the children and infants mostly born in New Zealand. While the overall health and wellbeing of this population was still reminiscent of its British/European origins, it was on the cusp of improvements that would take decades to be fully realised, but were slowly appearing. The role of the friendly societies would slowly develop until they were made almost instantly redundant by the passing of the *Social Security Act* of 1938, and medical science in the twentieth century would advance in leaps and bounds to improve all aspects of health. A nationwide infant mortality rate of 126 per 1000 live births in 1876 would permanently drop to below 100 by 1883, and would decline to 51 in 1920, 28 in 1950 and 6 in 2000 (https://teara. govt.nz/en/graph/30308/new-zealand-infant-mortality-rate-1862-2017). The people from St. John's Cemetery that have been discussed here had laid the foundations for a better life for their descendants, although arguably it was their grandchildren and great grandchildren rather than their children who experienced this.

References

Ancient Order of Foresters (1898) *General Laws for the Government of the Wellington District of the Ancient Order of Foresters' Friendly Society.* Wellington.

Andrews, J. (2009) *No Other Home Than This. A History of European New Zealanders.* Craig Potton Publishing, Nelson.

Anson, T.J. and Henneberg, M. (2004) A solution for the permanent storage of historical skeletal remains for research purposes: A South Australian precedent that keeps scientists and the Church community happy. *Australian Archaeology,* No. 58: 15-18.

Appendices to the Journals of the House of Representatives 1881, H-7: 2.

Arden, N. and M. Nevitt (2006). Osteoarthritis: Epidemiology. *Best Practice and Research Clinical Rheumatology* 20(1): doi:http://dx.doi.org/10.1016/j.berh.2005.1009.1007.

Ballantyne, T. (2012) *Webs of Empire: Locating New Zealand's Colonial Past.* Bridget Williams Books.

Beck, J., et al. (2000). Oral disease, cardiovascular disease and systemic inflammation. *Periodontology.* 23(1): 110-120.

Bedford, S. (1986) *The History and Archaeology of the Halfway House Hotel Site, Cromwell Gorge.* New Zealand Historic Places Trust, Cromwell.

Belich, J. (1996) *Making Peoples. A History of the New Zealanders from Polynesian Settlement to the End of the Nineteenth Century.* Penguin Books, Auckland.

Best. S., Furey, L. (2006) 'Westney Road Denominational Graveyard.' Unpublished report to the New Zealand Historic Places Trust. Downloaded from www.cfgheritage.com

Brickley, M., S. Buteux, J. Adams and R. Cherrington (2006) *St Martin's uncovered: investigations in the churchyard of St Martin's in-the-Bullring, Birmingham, 2001.* Oxbow Books, Oxford.

Brousil, J. and J. Hunter (2013). Femoral fractures in children. *Current Opinion in Pediatrics.* 25(1): 52-57.

Bruce Herald (newspaper, Milton) 13 July 1865, 29 November 1866, 19 February 1868, 27 January 1874, 15 June 1875, 11 September 1877.

Buckley, H. R., Roberts, P., Kinaston, R., Petchey, P., King, C., Domett, K., Snoddy, A. M., and Matisoo-Smith, E. (2020). Living and dying on the edge of the Empire: A bioarchaeological examination of Otago's early European settlers. *Journal of the Royal Society of New Zealand.* Advance online publication.

Buikstra, J.E. and Ubelaker, D.H. (1994) *Standards for Data Collection from Human Skeletal Remains.* Fayetteville: Arkansas Archaeological Survey.

Burns, P. (1989) *Fatal Success. A History of the New Zealand Company.* Heinemann Reed, Auckland.

Campbell, M., et al. (2013) Introduction: An Archaeology for the Modern World. In, *Finding Our Recent Past, Historical Archaeology in New Zealand.* M. Campbell, S. Holdaway, and S. Macready, Editors. New Zealand Archaeological Association Monograph No. 29: Auckland: pp1-8.

Campbell, M., Furey, L. (2013) Identity in Rural Mangere. In, *Finding Our Recent Past, Historical Archaeology in New Zealand.* M. Campbell, S. Holdaway, and S. Macready, Editors. New Zealand Archaeological Association Monograph No. 29: Auckland: pp123-142.

Cemetery Reserves Ordinance 1864. Otago Ordinances, Session XVIII, No. 145, 1864

Cemetery Reserves Management Ordinance 1864. Otago Ordinances, Session XVIII, No. 146, 1864

Clarke R, Topley E., Fear C. (1955) Assessment of blood-loss in civilian trauma. *The Lancet.* 268 (6865): 629–638.

Clarke, A. (2012) *Born to a Changing World: Childbirth in Nineteenth Century New Zealand.* Bridgit Williams Books Ltd, Wellington.

Cowie, R., Bekvalac, J., Kausmally, T. (2008) *Late 17th to 19th century burial and earlier occupation at All Saints, Chelsea Old Church, Royal Borough of Kensington and Chealsea.* Museum of London Archaeology Service, MOLAS Archaeology Studies Series 18.

Deed, S. (2015) *Unearthly Landscapes. New Zealand's early cemeteries, churchyards and urupā.* Otago University Press, Dunedin.

Deetz, J.F. (1967) 'Death's Head, Cherub, Urn and Willow.' *Natural History* 79 (3): 29-37.

Domett, K., et al. (2017). Interpreting osteoarthritis in bioarchaeology: Highlighting the importance of a clinical approach through case studies from prehistoric Thailand. *Journal of Archaeological Science: Reports.* 11: 762-773.

Donlon, D., Griffin, R., Casey, M., (2017) The Old Sydney Burial Ground: clues from the dentition about the ancestry, health and diet of the first British settlers of

Australia. *Australasian Historical Archaeology*, 35: 43-53.

Dougherty, I. (2017) *Dunedin. Founding a New World City*. Saddle Hill Press, Dunedin.

Eldred-Grigg, S. (1984) *Pleasures of the Flesh. Sex and Drugs in Colonial New Zealand 1840-1915*. A.H. and A.W. Reed Ltd., Wellington.

Ell, G., Ell, S. (1995) *Great Journeys in Old New Zealand. Travel and exploration in a new land.* The Bush Press, Auckland.

Elwood P. (1965) Respiratory symptoms in men who had previously worked in a flax mill in Northern Ireland. *British Journal of Industrial Medicine.* 22:38–42.

Findlay, R., Michelle, I., Crow, K., Miller, M., Galletly, V. (2015) 'A History of the St. John's Burial Ground, Back Road, Tokomairiro, Otago.' R.M. Findlay, Auckland.

Foster, A., et al. (2014). Using Enthesis robusticity to infer activity in the past: A review. *Journal and Archaeological Method and Theory.* 21: 511-533.

Fraser, A.J.T. (1941) *History of St. John's Church, Milton, 1858-1941.* Compiled on the occasion of the 75th Anniversary of the Dedication of St. John's Church. Milton.

Fraser, L., McCarthy, A. (eds) (2012) *Far From Home, The English in New Zealand.* Otago University Press, Dunedin.

Fraser, L. (2012) 'Memory, Mourning and Melancholy. English Ways of Death on the Margins of Empire.' In, Fraser, L., McCarthy, A. (eds) *Far From 'Home,' The English in New Zealand.* Otago University Press.

Fulton, R. (1922). *Medical Practice in Otago and Southland in the Early Days: A description of the manner of life, trials, and difficulties of some of the pioneer doctors, of the places in which, and of the people among whom they laboured.* Dunedin, Otago Daily Times and Witness Newspapers Co. Ltd.

Garland, J. (2013) 'Medicating Miners: Historical Archaeology of the St. Bathans Cottage Hospital.' MA thesis, University of Otago.

Gowland, R., Caffell, A., Newman, S., Levene, A., Holst, M. (2018a). Broken Childhoods: Rural and Urban non-adult health during the Industrial Revolution in Northern England (Eighteenth–Nineteenth Centuries). *Bioarchaeology International.* 2(1): 44-62.

Gowland R. (2018b) 'A mass of crooked alphabets': the construction and othering of working class bodies in industrial England. In: Stone PK, editor. *Bioarchaeological analyses and bodies, bioarchaeology: New ways of knowing anatomical and archaeological skeletal collections.* Cham (Switzerland): Springer International Publishing; p. 147–160.

Gurr, A., Kumaratilake, J., Brrok, A.H., Loannou, S., Pate, F.D., Henneberg, M. (2022) Health effects of European colonization: An investigation of skeletal remains from 19th to early 20th century migrant settlers in South Australia. *Plos One*, 17(4).

Harper, M. (2012) 'Everything is English.' Expectations, Experiences and Impacts of English Migrants to New Zealand, 1840-1970. In, Fraser, L., McCarthy, A. (eds) *Far From Home, The English in New Zealand.* Otago University Press, Dunedin.

Hillson, S. (1996) *Dental Anthropology.* Cambridge: Cambridge University Press.

Hillson, S. (2008). Dental pathology. *Biological Anthropology of the Human Skeleton.* M. A. Katzenberg and S. Saunders. New York, Wiley-Liss.

Hocken, T.M. (1898) *Contributions to the Early History of New Zealand. (Settlement of Otago).* Sampson, Low, Marston and Company, London.

Hoile, S. (2018) Coffin furniture in London c. 1700-1850: the establishment of tradition in the material culture of the grave. *Post-Medieval Archaeology.* 52 (2): 210-223.

Holland, P. (2013) *Home in the Howling Wilderness. Settlers and the Environment in Southern New Zealand.* Auckland University Press.

Huck, P. (1995) Infant Mortaility and Living Standards of English Workers During the Industrial Revolution. *The Journal of Economic History*, Vol. 55, No. 3, pp 528-550.

Hutton, F.W. (1875) *Report on the Geology and Goldfields of Otago.* Mills, Dick and Co., Dunedin.

Jones, M. (2012) 'Dalmatian Settlement and Identity in New Zealand: the Devcich Farm, Kauaeranga Valley, near Thames.' *Australasian Historical Archaeology*, 30, 2012: 24-33.

Katzenberg, M.A. and S. Saunders, eds. (2008) *Biological Anthropology of the Human Skeleton.* Wiley-Liss: Hoboken, New Jersey.

King, C., Buckley, H.R., Petchey, P., Kinaston, R., Millard, A., Zech, J., Patrick Roberts, P., Matisoo-Smith, E., Nowell, G., Gröcke, D.R. (2020). A multi-isotope, multi-tissue study of colonial origins and diet in New Zealand. *American Journal of Physical Anthropology.* 172: 605-620.

King, C., Buckley, H., Petchey, P., Roberts, P., Zech, J., Kinaston, R., Collins, C., Kardailsky, O., Matisoo-Smith, E. and Nowell, G. (2021a). An isotopic and genetic study of multi-cultural colonial New Zealand. *Journal of Archaeological Science,* 128: 105337.

King, C., Petchey, P., Kinaston, R., Gröcke, D., Millard, A., Wanhalla, A., Brooking, T., Matisoo-Smith, E. and Buckley, H. (2021b). A Land of Plenty? Colonial Diet in Rural New Zealand. *Historical Archaeology.,* 55: doi.org/10.1007/s41636-020-00276-y.

Lake County Press (newspaper, Arrowtown) 31 December 1885.

Larsen, C. (2002) *Bioarchaeology: the lives and lifestyles of past people.* J. Archaeol. Res.. 10(2): p. 119-166.

Lavery, M., Huang, M., Amendola, A. (2007) Plastic deformity in a 9-year-old boy. *Clinical Orthopaedics and Related Research.* 462: 238-241.

Lowe, A., Mackay, R. (1992) Old Sydney Burial Ground. *Australasian Historical Archaeology*, Vol. 10: 15-23.

McDonald, K.C. (1965) *City of Dunedin.* Dunedin City Corporation, Dunedin.

MacBean Stewart F. (1875) 'Medical Officer of Health, Milton, to His Worship the Mayor'. Reports from the Boards of Health in the Various Provinces, H-22, *Appendices to the Journals of the House of Representatives.*

Mackintosh, T. (1966) *Centennial History 1866-1966. The Parish of St. John the Evangelist, Milton.*

Mahoney-Swales, D., O'Neill, R., Willmott, H (2011) The Hidden Material Culture of Death: Coffins and Grave Goods in Late 18th- and Early 19th-Century Sheffield. In, King, C and Sayer, D. (eds) *The Archaeology of Post-Medieval Religion.* Boydell Press.

Marshall, P. (1918) *The Geology of the Tuapeka District.* New Zealand Department of Mines, Geological Survey Branch, Bulletin No. 19 (New Series). Government Printer, Wellington.

Mataura Ensign (newspaper, Gore) 15 October 1889.

Miles, A., Connell, B. (2012) *New Bunhill Fields Burial Ground, Southwark. Excavations at the Globe Academy, 2008.* Archaeology Study Series 24. Museum of London Archaeology, London.

Mohammadien, H., Hussein, M., El-Sokkary, R. (2013). Effects of exposure to flour dust on respiratory symptoms and pulmonary function of mill workers. *Egyptian Journal of Chest Diseases and Tuberculosis.* 62: 745-753.

Moorrees, C. F. A., Fanning, E.A., Hunt, E.E. (1963). Age variation of formation stages for ten permanent teeth. *Journal of Dental Research.* 42: 1490-1502.

Moorrees, C. F. A., et al. (1963). Formation and resorption of three deciduous teeth in children. *American Journal of Physical Anthropology.* 21: 205-213.

Mount Ida Chronicle (newspaper, Naseby) 3 October 1902.

Mytum, H. (2003) 'Death and Remembrance in the Colonial Context,' in Lawrence (ed) *Archaeologies of the British, Explorations of Identity in Great Britain and its Colonies 1600-1945.* Routledge, London, pp 156-173.

Olssen, E. (1984) *A History of Otago.* John McIndoe, Dunedin.

Olsse, E. (1996) 'Friendly Societies in New Zealand, 1840-1990.' In, M. van der Linden (ed) *Social Security Mutualism, The Comparative History of Mutual Benefit Societies.* Peter Lang AG, Berne.

Ortner, D. (Ed.) (2003). *Identification of Pathological Conditions in Human Skeletal Remains.* USA, Academic Press.

Otago Provincial Government Gazette, Vol. X No. 407, 14 February 1866; Vol. X No. 457, 31 December 1866

Otago Witness (newspaper, Dunedin) 1 February 1894

Owen, T., Casey, M. (2017) The Old Sydney Burial Ground: using isotopic analysis to infer the origin of individual skeletons. *Australasian Historical Archaeology*, 35: 24-33.

Owen, T., Casey, M., Pitt, N. (2017) The Old Sydney Burial Ground: an inference of early colonial diet in Sydney and Britain. *Australasian Historical Archaeology*, 35: 34-42

Palenski, R. (2012) *The Making of New Zealanders.* Auckland University Press, Auckland.

Pearson, A., Jeffs, B., Witkin, A., MacQuarrie, H. (2011) *Infernal Traffic: Excavation of a Liberated African Graveyard in Rupert's Valley, St. Helena.* Council for British Archaeology Research report 169.

Petchey, P.G., Innanchai, J. (2012) Bottle Top Capsules in New Zealand Historic Archaeological Sites. *Journal of Pacific Archaeology.* Vol. 3 (2): 1-16.

Petchey, P.G., Brosnahan, S. (2016) 'Finding Meaning and Identity in New Zealand Buildings Archaeology: The Example of 'Parihaka' House, Dunedin.' *Journal of Pacific Archaeology.* Vol. 7 (2): 26-42.

Petchey, P.G. (2018) 'First Footsteps in a New World City: The Dunedin causeway and early settlers' adaptation to their new home.' *Historical Archaeology*, 52 (4): 700-716.

Petchey, P., Buckley, H., Hil, G., Kelly, A., Kinaston, R., King, C., Scott, R. (2018) 'Life and Death on the Otago Frontier. Preliminary Report on the Lawrence Cemeteries. *Archaeology in New Zealand*, 61(2): 22-40.

Petchey, P.G., Buckley, H., Scott, R. (2018) Life, Death and Care on the Otago Goldfields: A Preliminary Glimpse. *Journal of Pacific Archaeology,* Vol. 9 (2): 44-58.

Petchey, P., Buckley, H., Kinaston, R., Smith, B. (2017) 'A Nineteenth Century Settlers' Graveyard: Preliminary report on the excavation of St. John's Cemetery, Back Road, Milton, Otago.' *Archaeology in New Zealand*, 60(1):19-30.

Phillips, J., Hearn, T. (2008) *Settlers. New Zealand Immigrants from England, Ireland and Scotland, 1800-1945.* Auckland University Press, Auckland.

Pitt, N., Casey, M., Lowe, A., Stocks, R. (2017) The Old Sydney Burial Ground: The 2008 archaeological investigations. *Australasian Historical Archaeology*, Vol. 35: 3-23.

Pool I. (1991) *Te Iwi Māori: a New Zealand population past, present and projected.* Auckland: Auckland University Press.

Pool I. (2015) *Colonization and development in New Zealand between 1769 and 1900: the seeds of Rangiatea.* Charbit Y, Pool I, editors. Switzerland: Springer.

Price, T., Burton, J., Bentley, R. (2002) *The characterization of biologically available strontium isotope ratios for the study of prehistoric migration.* Archaeometry, 44(1): p. 117-135.

Prickett, N. (1994) *Archaeological Excavations at the Omata Stockade and Warea Redoubt, Taranaki.* New Zealand Archaeological Association Monograph No. 20.

Richie, A. (1997) 'Johnny Come Lately': Chinese Miners on the Cenral Otago Goldfields. In, Trotter, M. McCullloch, B. (1997) *Digging up the Past, New Zealand's Archaeological History.* Viking, Penguin Books (NZ) Ltd., Auckland.

Roberts, C.A., Cox, M. (2003) *Health and Disease in Britain: From Prehistory to the Present Day.* Gloucester, Sutton Publishing.

Roberts, C. and K. Manchester (2005). The Archaeology of Disease. Ithaca, N.Y., Cornell University Press.

Roberts, P. (2006). 'Gold Fever.Disease and its Cultural Relationship:A Case Study on the Development of the Colony of Victoria, 1950 to 1900.' The Australian National University. Master of Arts.

Rocco, F. (2003) *The Miraculous Fever-Tree. The Cure That Changed the World.* Harper Collins, London.

Schama, S. (2002) *A History of Britain. Volume 3, The Fate of Empire 1776-2000.* BBC Worldwide Ltd., London.

Scheuer, L., Black, S. (2000). *Developmental Juvenile Osteology.* London, Academic Press

Smith, I. (2004) 'Archaeologies of Identity: Historical Archaeology for the 21st Century.' In, Furey, L., Holdaway, S. (eds) *Change Through Time: 50 Years of New Zealand Archaeology.* New Zealand Archaeological Association Monograph No. 26.

Smith, I. (2008) 'Maori, Pakeha and Kiwi: Peoples, culture and sequence in New Zealand archaeology.' In Clark, G., Leach, F., O'Connor, S. (eds) *Islands of Inquiry.* Terra Australis 29, Australian National University.

Smith, I. (2019) *Pākehā Settlements in a Māori World. New Zealand Archaeology 1769-1860.* Bridget Williams Books, Wellington.

Snoddy, A.M.E., Buckley, H. R., King, C. L., Kinaston, R. L., Nowell, G., Gröcke, D. R., Duncan, W. J., and

Petchey, P. (2019). 'Captain of All These Men of Death': An integrated case study of tuberculosis in nineteenth-century Otago, New Zealand. *Bioarchaeology International, 3*(4).

Snoddy, A.M.E., King, C., Petchey, P., Miszkiewicz, J., Kinaston, R., Bucklet, H. (2021) 'Disability and Difference on the New Zealand Frontier: Possible Skeletal Dysplasia in Nineteenth-Century Milton, Otago.' Bioarchaeology International, Vol. 5 No. 2.

Soper, E.L. (1948) *The Otago of our Mothers.* Otago Centennial Historical Publications.

Sumpter, D.J., Lewis, J.J. (1949) *Faith and Toil. The Story of Tokomairiro.* Otago Centennial Historical Publications.

Thomas, T., Stewart, P. (1987). Mortality from lung cancer and respiratory disease among pottery workers exposed to silica and talc. *American Journal of Epidemiology.* 125 (1): 35-43.

Tilley, L., Oxenham, M. (2011) 'Survival Against the Odds: Modeling the Social Implications of Care Provision to Serious Disables Individuals.' *International Journal of Paleopathology* Vol. 1, 35-42.

Tilley, L. (2015) *Theory and Practice in the Bioarchaeology of Care.* Springer International.

Trotter, M., Gleser, G. (1952). Estimation of stature from long bones of American Whites and Negroes. *American Journal of Physical Anthroplogy.* 10(4): 463-514.

Trotter, M., Gleser, G. (1958). A re-evaluation of estimation of stature based on measurements of stature taken during life and of long bones after death. *American Journal of Physical Anthroplogy* 16: 79-123.

Trotter, M., McCulloch, B. (1989) 'Historical Records or Archaeological Facts? The Withell's Road Cemetery.' *New Zealand Journal of Archaeology,* Volume 11, pp5-21.

Tuapeka Times (newspaper, Lawrence) 10 October 1872

Vaccination Act 1863. (New Zealand legislation)

Wedel, V. and A. Galloway (2014). *Broken Bones: Anthroplogical Analysis of Blunt Force Trauma.* Proquest Ebook Central, Charles C. Thomas Publisher.

West, J. (2017) *The Face of Nature. An Environmental History of the Otago Peninsula.* Otago University Press, Dunedin.

Wise's New Zealand Post Office Directory 1875-1876

Worksafe New Zealand (2016) *Good Practice Guidelines: Excavation Safety.* New Zealand Government, Wellington.

Manuscript and Archival Sources

Higgins, Joseph. Canada Reef near Tokomairiro. Archives New Zealand, Dunedin Regional Office. DAAC D256 18116 Box 538.

Otago Deeds 4/491, 29/232, 86/484 (Archives New Zealand, Dunedin Regional Office).

SO 7357 (1897) Land Information New Zealand.

Otago Deeds Plan 309 (1909) Land Information New Zealand.

Websites

www.ancestrylibrary.com.au

www.kaelewis.com :based on: Miner's Rights Registration Book and Business Licenses, Tuapeka, Otago: ATL Ref: qms-2045 Manuscript: 0713 (19 August - 1 November 1861).

https://www.mindat.org/loc-299936.html

https://teara.govt.nz/en/graph/30308/new-zealand-infant-mortality-rate-1862-2017

https://teara.govt.nz/en/marriage-and-partnering/page-2

https://www.thegazette.co.uk/London/issue/21758/page/3021/data.pdf

Appendix

A.1. Fabric Analysis

Table A.1. Identification of the fabric structures, yarn structures and fibre contents of archaeological textile fragments from Milton Cemetery.

Fragment bag labels				Identification through microscopy		
Burial		**Context #**	**Description**	**Fabric structure**	**Yarn structure**	**Fibre content**
SJM 2016	1	Context # 10013	coffin cloth	2/1 twill weave (finely woven) The wool yarn predominates on the fabric face, but warp and weft yarn designations are not certain.	wa: single, z-spun we: single, z-spun	wa: fine wool we: cotton, highly degraded
SJM 2016	2	Context # 10005	coffin cloth lid fabric (sample 1)	plain weave, heavily fulled (thickened through felting). One set of yarns predominates over the fabric surface on both sides. Other set seems to be decomposed.	main yarn: single, z-spun	main yarn: fine and coarse wool, some with fragmented medulla. Can see dyed fibres blended together (blue, green, red and natural).
SJM 2016	B2	Context # 10005	coffin cloth (side) (sample 2)	2/2 twill	wa: single, z-spun we: single, z-spun	wa: fine wool, can see some scales. we: fine wool can see some scales.
SJM 2016	3a	Context # 10006	coffin lid fabric	2/2 twill	wa: single, z-spun we: single, z-spun	wa: fine wool, can see some scales. we: fine wool, can see many scales.
SJM 2016	3b	Context # 10019	coffin fabric	2/2 twill	wa: single, z-spun we: single, z-spun	wa: fine wool, faint trace of scales. we: fine wool, faint trace of scales. Fibres appear to be dyed black.
SJM 2016	4	Context # 10018	coffin fabric	plain weave, heavily fulled so that woven structure is obscured.	main yarn: single, z-spun; other yarn not separated from felted structure.	main yarn: wool fibres; can see blue, red and natural-coloured, various sizes, faint scales.
SJM 2016	5	Context # 10012	coffin fabric	plain weave, napped or brushed on one side; weave is somewhat obscured by pile fibres.	main yarn: single, z-spun; other yarn not separated from brushed structure.	main yarn: wool fibres; can see blue, red and natural-coloured, various sizes, faint scales.
SJM 2016	6	Context # 10016	coffin fabric	plain weave napped or brushed on one side; weave is somewhat obscured by pile fibres.	main yarn: single, z-spun; other yarn not separated from brushed structure.	main yarn: wool fibres; can see blue, red and natural-coloured, various sizes, faint scales. Fine and course fibres some with fragmented medulla.
SJM 2016	7	Context # 10014	coffin fabric	2/1 twill weave (finely woven). The wool yarn predominates on the fabric face, but warp and weft yarn designations are not certain.	wa: single, z-spun we: single z-spun	wa: fine wool we: cotton, highly degraded.
SJM 2016	7	Context # 10014	clothing fabric? (fabric tape)	fabric tape: narrow braid (oblique interlacing).	yarns: 2-ply, zzS-spun	yarns: fine and course wool in poor condition (can see some fibres with medulla) all white.
SJM 2016	7	Context # 10014	clothing fabric? (cloth with raised nap)	cloth with raised nap: plain weave, heavily fulled and napped or brushed	main yarn: single, z-spun; other yarn not separated from brushed structure.	main yarn: wool fibres; can see blue, red, natural-coloured and maybe black, various sizes, faint scales, poor condition.
SJM 2016	9	Context # 10015	clothing fabric	2/2 twill weave, fabric is fulled but not napped	wa: single, s-spun we: single, s-spun	wa: fine wool, poor condition, can see some scales we: fine wool, poor condition can see some scales.

91

Fragment bag labels				Identification through microscopy		
Burial		**Context #**	**Description**	**Fabric structure**	**Yarn structure**	**Fibre content**
SJM 2016	B9	Context # 10015	coffin fabric	2/2 twill, finely woven; traces of selvedge. Warp yarns are used in pairs and form 5 vertical ribs next to the finished edge of the fabric.	wa: single, z-spun we: single, z-spun	wa: fine wool, poor condition, can see some scales. we: fine wool poor condition can see some scales.
SJM 2016	10	Context # 10028	coffin lid fabric	2/1 twill The wool yarn predominates on the fabric face, but warp and weft yarn designations are not certain.	wa: single, z-spun we: single, z-spun	wa: fine wool. we: cotton, highly degraded.
SJM 2016	11	Context # 10029	coffin side fabric	2/1 twill weave	wa: single, z-spun we: single, z-spun	wa: fine wool, can see some scales. we: fine wool, can see scales, some fibres may be dyed black.
SJM 2016	13	Context # 10026	coffin side fabric	2/2 twill weave (very fine fabric)	wa: single, z-spun we: single, z-spun	wa: fine wool, can see scales, fibres appear to be dyed black. we: fine wool, can see some scales, also appears to be dyed black.
SJM 2016	15	Context # 10042	cloth over burial	plain weave; open structure; poor condition - fragment folded on itself	wa: single, s-spun we: single, s-spun	wa: wool, highly degraded, some course fibres. we: wool, highly degraded, can't see scales.
SJM 2016	16	Context # 10043	coffin fabric	2/2 twill weave	wa: single, z-spun we: single, z-spun	wa: wool we: wool
SJM 2016	18	Context # 10044	coffin fabric	plain weave; only small area where cotton yarn is preserved and fabric structure maintained. Warp and weft yarn designations are not certain.	wa: single, z-spun we: single, s-spun	wa: fine wool (dark maybe dyed black). we: cotton highly degraded
SJM 2016	19	Context # 10045	coffin fabric	plain weave	wa: single, s-spun we: single, s-spun	wa: wool highly degraded some course fibres. we: wool; highly degraded can't see scales.
SJM 2016	20a	Context # 10046	coffin fabric	2/1 twill weave	wa: single, z-spun we: single, z-spun	wa: fine wool, can see some scales. we: fine wool, can see scales, some fibres may be dyed black.
SJM 2016	21	Context # 10047	coffin fabric	plain weave, heavily fulled so that woven structure is obscured; brushed on one side to form a nap.	main yarn, single, z-spun; other yarn not separated from brushed structure.	main yarn: wool of various sizes and some dark-coloured, red, black, blue.
SJM 2016	21	Context # 10047	ribbon across maxilla	fine, braided structure (oblique interlacement)	yarns: single, no twist, multifilament	main yarn: silk fibres, dyed bright blue (not able to separate fibres in yarn without breaking them).
SJM 2016	22	Context # 10048	coffin fabric	plain weave, only one set of yarns remains (might be weft)	yarns: single, z-spun	main yarn: wool of various sizes, poor condition, some evidence of scales.
SJM 2016	27	Context # 10053	coffin fabric	2/2 twill weave (green fabric)	wa: single, z-spun we: single, z-spun	wa: fine wool, faint trace of scales. we: fine wool faint trace of scales; all fibres dyed blue although fabric looks green.
SJM 2016	28	Context # 10056	coffin lid fabric	2/2 twill weave tan brown	wa: single, z-spun we: single, z-spun	wa: fine wool, faint trace of scales. we: fine wool faint trace of scales.
SJM 2016	29	Context # 10057	coffin fabric	2/2 twill weave	wa: single, z-spun we: single, z-spun	wa: wool of various sizes, can see some scales, fibres may be dyed black. we: wool of various sizes, can see scales, some fibres may be dyed black.

Table A.2. Images of fabric structures (warp yarns oriented vertically in most instances) and fibres present in warp and weft yarns.

Burial 1: 2/1 twill weave	Wool fibres in warp yarn	
Burial 2 (sample 1): plain weave	Wool fibres in preserved yarn (warp)	Cotton fibres in weft yarn
Burial B2 (sample 2): 2/2 twill weave	Wool fibres in warp yarn	Wool fibres in preserved yarn (warp)
		Wool fibres in weft yarn

Burial 3a: 2/2 twill weave

Wool fibres in warp yarn

Wool fibres in weft yarn

Burial 3b: 2/2 twill weave

Wool fibres in warp yarn

Wool fibres in weft yarn

Burial 4: plain weave (fulled and napped)

Wool fibres in preserved yarn (warp or weft)

Wool fibres in preserved yarn (warp or weft)

Wool fibres in preserved yarn (warp or weft)

Wool fibres in preserved yarn (warp or weft)

Wool fibre in preserved yarn (warp or weft)

Cotton fibre in weft yarn

Wool fibres in preserved yarn (warp or weft)

Wool fibres in preserved yarn (warp or weft)

Wool fibre in warp yarn

Burial 5: plain weave (fulled and napped)

Burial 6 plain weave (fulled and napped)

Burial 7: 2/1 twill weave

Wool fibres in braiding yarns

Wool fibres in braiding yarns

Burial 7: Braid (finished edge on R-side)

Wool fibres in preserved yarn (warp or weft)

Wool fibres in preserved yarn (warp or weft)

Burial 7: plain weave (fulled and napped)

Wool fibres in weft yarn

Wool fibres in warp yarn

Burial 9: 2/2 twill weave (fulled)

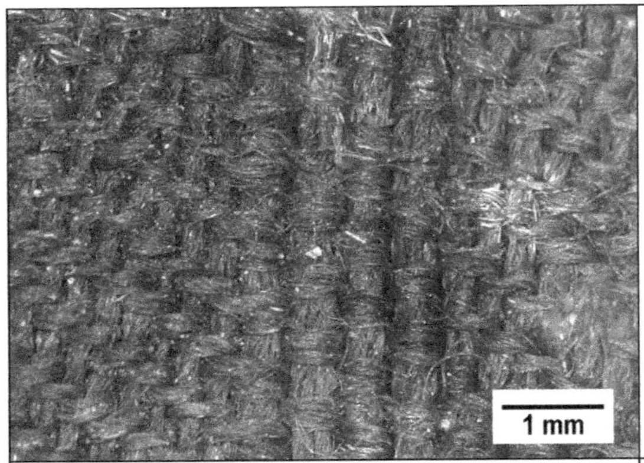

Wool fibres in weft yarn

Wool fibres in warp yarn

Burial B9: 2/2 twill weave near selvedge

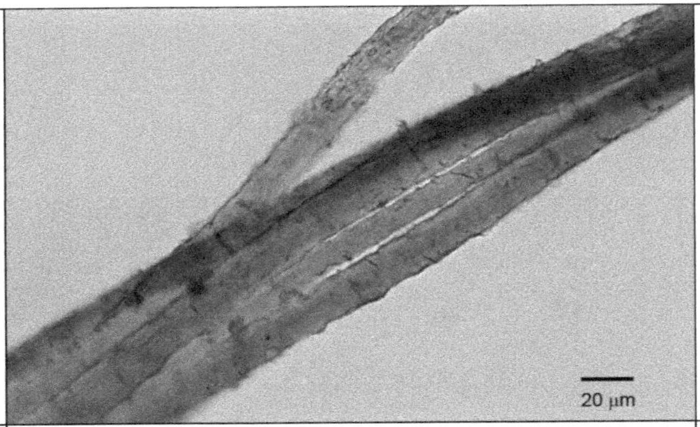

Wool fibres in weft yarn

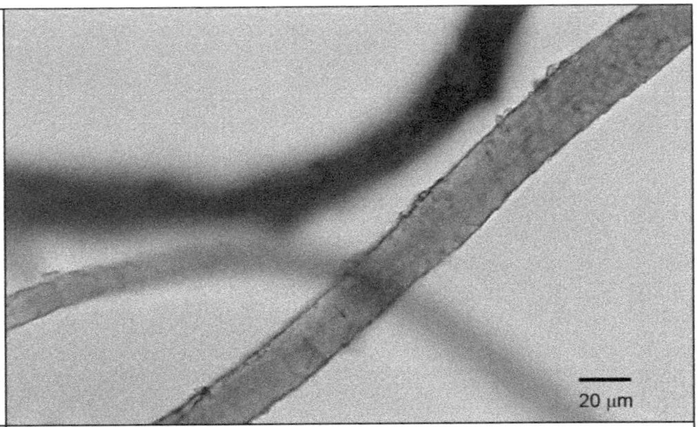

Wool fibres in warp yarn

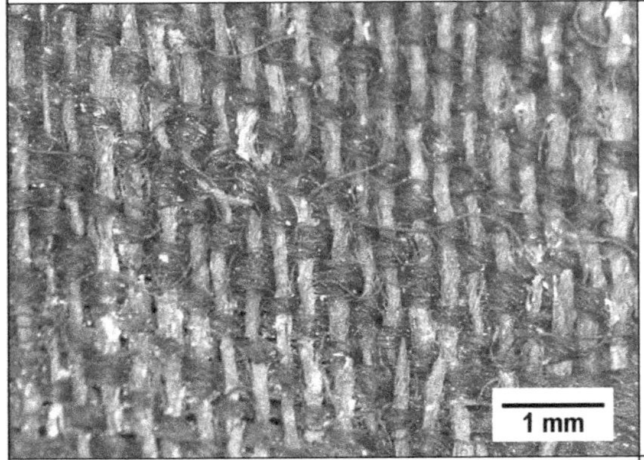

Burial 10: 2/1 twill (cotton yarns shown vertically in image)

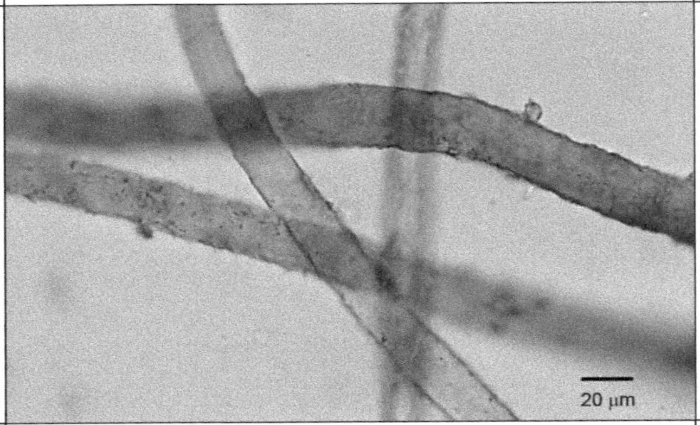

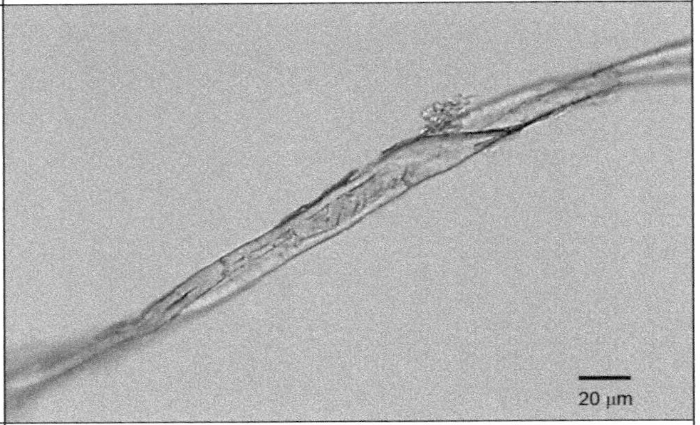

Cotton fibres in weft yarn

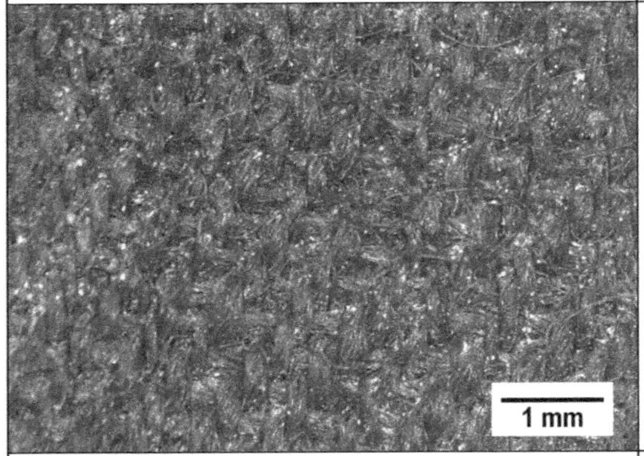

Wool fibres in warp yarn

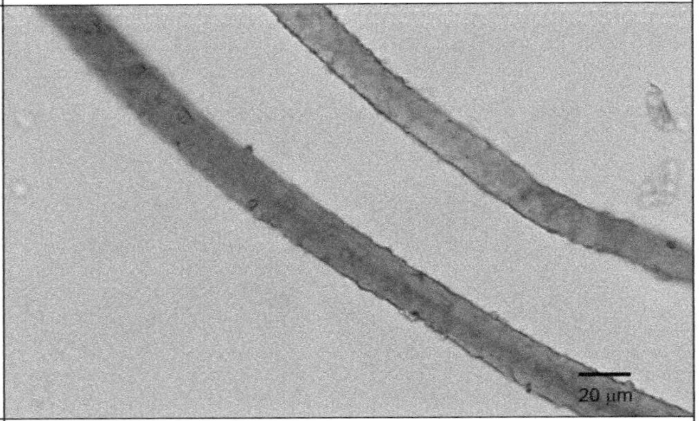

Wool fibres in weft yarn

Wool fibres in warp yarn

Burial 11: 2/1 twill weave

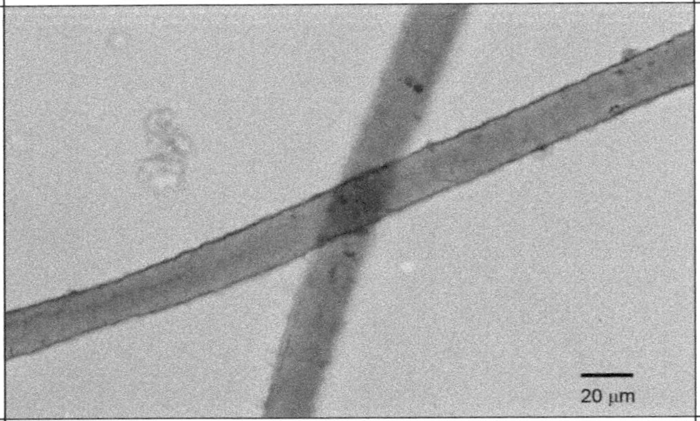

Burial 13: 2/2 twill weave — Wool fibres in warp yarn — Wool fibres in weft yarn

Burial 15: plain weave — Wool fibres in warp yarn — Wool fibres in weft yarn

Burial 16: 2/2 twill weave — Wool fibres in warp yarn — Wool fibres in weft yarn

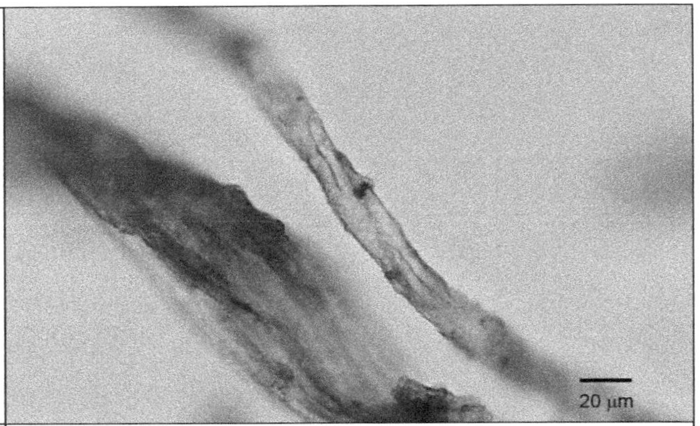

Cotton fibres in weft yarn

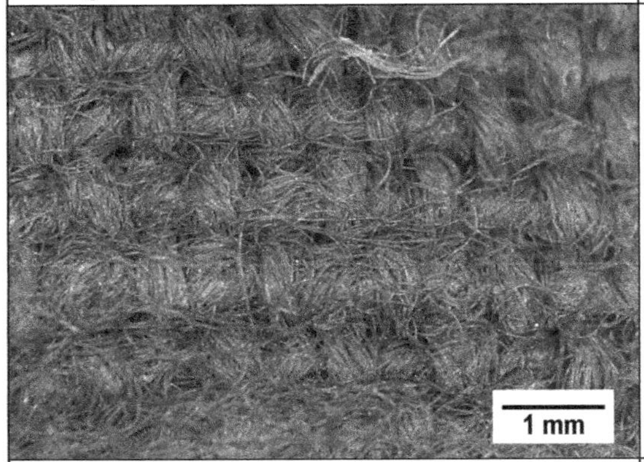

Wool fibres in warp yarn

Burial 18: plain weave (cotton yarns shown vertically in image)

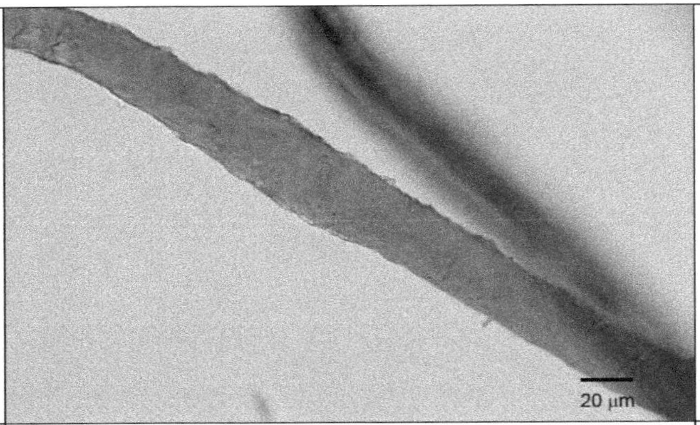

Wool fibres in weft yarn

Wool fibres in warp yarn

Burial 19: plain weave

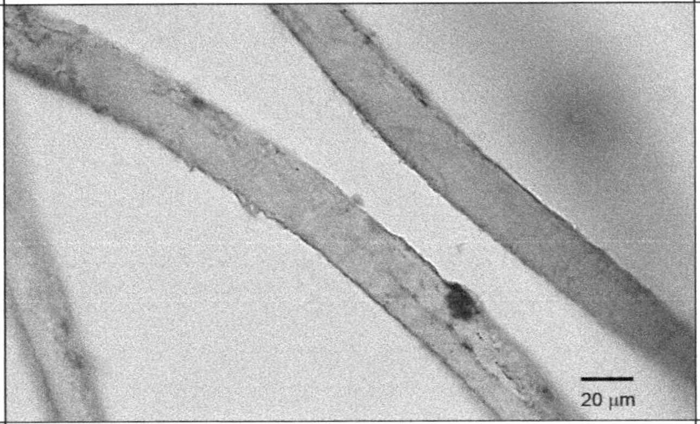

Wool fibres in weft yarn

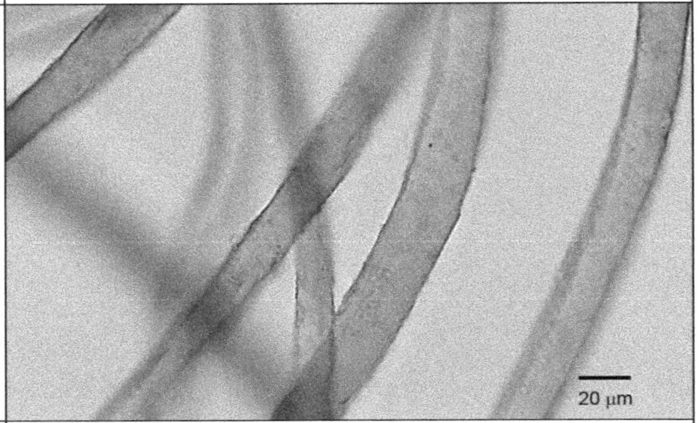

Wool fibres in warp yarn

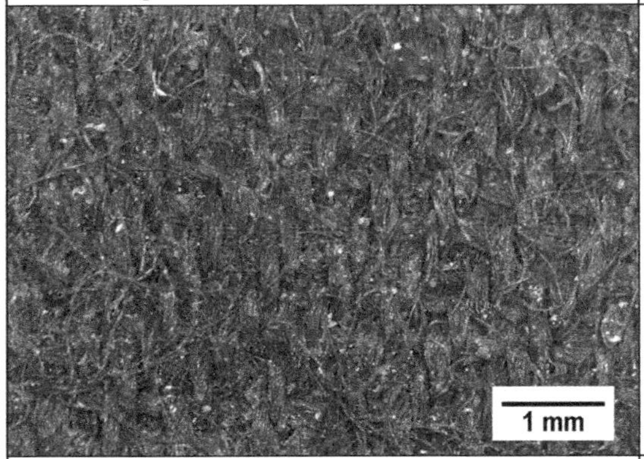

Burial 20a: 2/1 twill weave

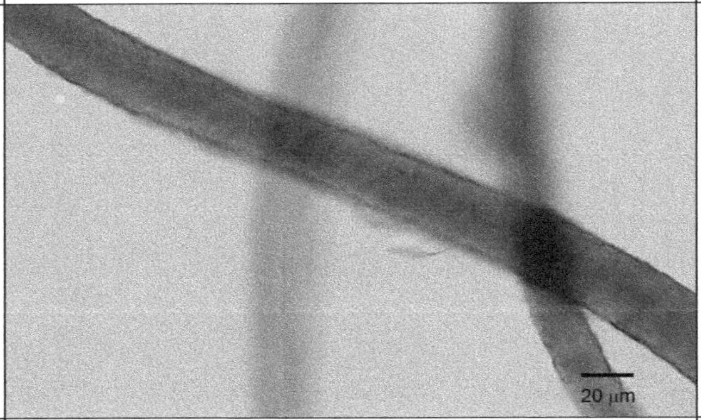

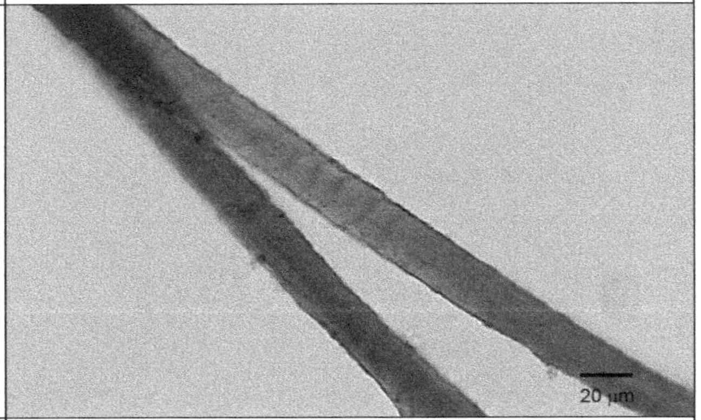

Burial 21 coffin fabric: plain weave — Wool fibres in preserved yarn (warp or weft) — Wool fibre in preserved yarn (warp or weft)

Burial 21 ribbon: braid — Silk fibres in braiding yarns — Silk fibres in braiding yarns

Burial 22: plain weave — Wool fibres in preserved yarn (warp or weft) — Wool fibre in preserved yarn (warp or weft)

Wool fibres in weft yarn

Wool fibres in weft yarn

Wool fibres in weft yarn

Wool fibres in warp yarn

Wool fibres in warp yarn

Wool fibres in warp yarn

Burial 27: 2/2 twill weave

Burial 28: 2/2 twill weave

Burial 29: 2/2 twill weave

www.ingramcontent.com/pod-product-compliance
Lightning Source LLC
Chambersburg PA
CBHW061006030426

42334CB00033B/3380